Parent Sense: Surviving Parenting And Helping You And Your Child Throughout Life

Parent Sense

Also by Stanley Goldstein
www.drstanleygoldstein.com

Nonfiction

Shopping For A Shrink: Finding The Right Psychotherapist For You Or Your Child

Troubled Children/Troubled Parents: The Way Out

Through Children's Minds: The Marketing And Creation Of Children's Products

Mental Health In A Minute: One-Hundred-And- One/One Minute Lessons To Improve Your Life

Fiction

Park West: A Novel Of Love And Murder And Forgiveness

Ghosts And Angels: How, During An Epoch Of Terror, Goodness Vanquished Evil And Restored Faith

Lies In Progress

Stanley Goldstein, Ph.D.

Parent Sense: Surviving Parenting And Helping You And Your Child Throughout Life

Wyston Books, Inc.

WYSTON BOOKS, INC.

E-mail: wystonbooks@yahoo.com
Please visit our website: www.wystonbooks.com

Goldstein, Stanley
Parent Sense: Surviving Parenting And
Helping You And Your Child Throughout Life

1.Parent and Child
2.Psychological Development

ISBN (E-book): 978-1-7376816-2-5
ISBN (Print): 978-1-7376816-3-2

Cover Photo by Catherine Delahaye/Digital Vision
Licensed from Getty Images

To parents, whose job takes longer
and is harder than mine.

Contents

Parent Sense

INTRODUCTION: MESSAGE TO PARENTS

Probably the most repeated phrase to new parents, apart from "things will get better" is "parenting isn't easy." Parents await the birth of their newborn, especially their first child, with a combination of anticipation and joy. Feelings that quickly turn to despair as sleepless nights and confusion ensue. The doctors and nurses did their part and now it's up to the parents.

But what can you do when your child won't sleep through the night or cries continually? They're certainly too young to understand or speak to. But are they?

Virtually sleepless, the mother of a three-year-old consulted me. Her daughter resisted going to bed and awoke continually throughout the night. Fearing this was caused by stomach distress, the mother consulted the girl's pediatrician who said that if the problem continued he would schedule tests.

I advised the mother that when a child wakes continually it's often because of scary dreams and how to speak with her daughter about them. I had earlier provided the mother a self-hypnotic relaxation audio which she occasionally listened to while holding her daughter. A week later the mother said that her daughter now slept through the night, falling asleep to the sound of my recorded voice. She told her mother, "I was scared."

To be sure, not every problem that a child presents can be so quickly alleviated with some requiring months or even years of treatment. But the more accurate information that parents possess about child development, the less stressful will be their parenting duties. My goal with this book is to ease their path so that joy may return to all.

Recognizing the harried lives of parents I have kept the essays that follow brief, each readable within two-minutes. But their length should not be confused with their value. Knowledge is the best antidote for anxiety, making the following pages priceless.

PART 1 - CHILDHOOD

MY BABY'S SLEEP PATTERN KEEPS ME AWAKE

While an adult's lack of sleep can create rash decisions and lowered immunity to illness, an almost universal cause follows the birth of their child. Which is understandable for just as a baby must quickly become accustomed to life outside their former protective womb, they now must pressure their parents to best meet their new needs. Which is difficult for their parents since the personality structure develops early in life and resists rapid change.

A healthy goal for all is having six to eight hours of sleep a night though this varies. A study of eminent scientists found theirs to range between four hours a night for Thomas Edison who took daily naps and twelve hours a night for Albert Einstein who didn't.

Getting enough sleep increases a mother's success in nursing and bonding with their baby which reduces the child's stress. It also reduces the risk of post-partum depression and helps maintain the marital relationship.

Babies may cry in the afternoon and evening for several reasons: they're too cold or too warm; they're tired or hungry; they need to burp or be changed. And there may be lengthy crying for apparently no reason when the baby seems pained though they are not and resists soothing. This peaks at about two months of age and lessens by five months.

It is critical that a baby bonds with their mother since a securely attached child experiences less stress which increases their ability to learn. What reduces this is abuse, pain, or lacking a responsive caregiver.

Admittedly, it is difficult for a baby's parent to get enough sleep without having a partner sharing the burden. Ideally, one goes to bed early and the other later so each is guaranteed at least five hours of continuous sleep. Daytime napping will help.

MY CHILD RESISTS GOING TO BED AND CONTINUALLY AWAKENS

It is normal that dreaming should frighten children since their mind is early in development. Assuming that no medical problems are awakening your child, you should explain dreaming to them as follows, speaking in a calm, even tone: "All dreams, even scary ones, are our good friends. They're like mystery movies that we make up to tell us what is going on inside us, maybe a happy trip we'll be going on. A scary dream is only telling you that you're doing you're afraid of, like maybe learning to ride or to swim. No dream can hurt you since they're all your good friends. When you wake up you can tell me your dream so we can figure out what it is telling you."

Repeating this in a reassuring tone each night will convince your child they aren't in danger when sleeping. Also, that if his parents aren't afraid of dreams they must be safe. It is the unconscious fear of their danger that keeps your child awake.

When frightened, a child may want to sleep with their parent(s) or in their room. This is normal too since fear paralyzes thinking and a child's mind is immature. Gradually encourage them to return to their bed, perhaps remaining until they are asleep.

Some children will refuse to sleep in their room, it having become associated with fear and anxiety. One eight-year-old boy slept on the living room sofa for a year until he could again consider his room safe. Each child has unique desires and temporary fears that need to be related to.

The unconscious is powerful, and one must respect its power. All children want to follow their parents' instructions since they *want* to behave in an adult fashion. When they're not it is because something is stopping them from doing so whether fatigue or illness or hunger or a belief making sense to them but not an adult.

Mature behavior is gained through development and not demand. The famed Swiss developmental psychologist, Jean Piaget, long insisted that nature has its own development schedule for a child and the process could not be speeded up. Though he added, Americans tend to ask, "How can we speed up the process?"

Thus, my advice to parents is to relax!

MY CHILD WETS THE BED

What doctors term *enuresis*, wetting the bed, is normal for babies and young children who have not yet gained full control of their bodies and learned social norms. But when persisting past the age of four and medical problems are absent, psychological factors should be considered. The human mind is complex and requires a long time to fully develop. Much behavior reflects the interaction of both physical and mental operations.

Consider how upset you feel while awaiting the results of a medical test. Normal anxiety symptoms often ensue: feeling hot or cold; having an elevated heart rate; experiencing pain at different parts of your body. All vanishing upon receiving positive news. A significant percentage of people rushing to a hospital's Emergency Room fearing that they are experiencing a heart attack are suffering only anxiety, which quickly disappears after receiving medical reassurance.

Psychologically, enuresis may reflect several conflicts. The child may be indirectly expressing their angry feelings by "pissing off their parents." Or they may want to regress to an earlier period of life when fewer demands for greater maturity of behavior were made.

Relieving this symptom, which is an embarrassment for all, involves communication and development, not edict. Being unconscious, this behavior is not controlled by your child who knows what they should do but cannot do it.

My suggestion is to speak to your child as follows, providing information which, slowly, will germinate in their conscious mind and enable bodily control. Say, in a soft, reassuring tone, "Sometimes when children wet the bed it's because they want to be young again. Which even grownups sometimes want and why they buy toys that they loved as children and collect comic books. A child may even be trying to say they're angry in this way. But this can't work since your mommy and daddy still won't know what is upsetting you. So, if something is bothering you, you'll have to tell us what it is."

Now your child won't be able, and you shouldn't expect it since musing about unconscious motives is hard even for adults. But, again, educating your child about themselves will ultimately increase their self-control.

If following this advice doesn't help within a tolerable period, professional help should be sought from a psychologist experienced with children. Note: if the doctor you consult cannot explain your child's unhappiness, which is what symptoms reflect, or uses jargon, another doctor should be consulted. And do trust your instincts with this decision just as you would when hiring any skilled worker.

MY CHILD SOILS THEIR PANTS

Among the most upsetting parenting experiences is when their child soils their pants. Not as a toddler before being toilet trained but afterward, when they know how to behave. Many parents, instructed by popular behavior modification (reward/punishment) concepts, punish their child without result. Nothing changes except for both being more distressed.

When not physically ill or having been toilet trained and after the age of four-years, children soil their pants not from inattention, over-involvement in an activity, as is often believed, but because they are unhappy. This symptom, the sign that something is wrong, is termed *encopresis*. Encopresis is unconsciously motivated and indicates the desire to regress, to return to an earlier period of life when greater maturity of behavior wasn't demanded. Basically, it is the desire to begin life anew.

Healing this symptom, which distresses the child as greatly as their parents, is accomplished by determining the reason for the child's unhappiness and remedying it, which usually requires professional aid.

If the soiling is recent and follows stress (as enrollment in a new school), it may quickly and spontaneously disappear without intervention and not reappear.

For a puzzling behavior to be considered a symptom it must both interfere with normal functioning and persist. As with medical symptoms, there is a logic to all mental health symptoms too. One develops a fever in response to infection. When the infection disappears so does the fever. Similarly, when a person's emotional distress ends, so too does their mental health symptom whether it be anxiety or depression or another.

MY CHILD HITS OR BITES

Infants and toddlers explore the world using their native capacities and skills which are their limbs and mouth and nose. To a newborn all occurrences arise from within them, from their experiences. Only gradually do these develop into a mind with its distinction between inside and outside oneself.

When a young child is angry it is normal for them to strike out by biting or hitting or throwing something. A parent's task is to educate their child, explaining they will feel better by speaking of their distress rather than acting-out. "If you tell me what is bothering you, I can help you but if you throw something or hit me or bite me I won't know what is bothering you and can't help you feel better," the parent should say.

While a toddler's potentially harmful or destructive behavior may reflect anger, they should not be considered acceptable for reasons of safety. And because children tend not to believe that a parent is serious unless they're emotional, drama is an important element when communicating during these situations. The parent should not fear to raise their voice, to speak vociferously when encountering inexcusable behavior. "What are you doing? You hurt me!" they should cry when their child hits or bites. "If I'm angry, can I bite or hit you?" they should ask. And disregard the child's response (which may be "yes") since children are often illogical and arguing with a troubled illogical child is a lost cause.

With greater maturity the behavior of most children will improve since they want to be an adult too. So they will do as their parents request unless something keeps them from it which could be illness, tiredness, hunger, or an emotional reason making sense to them but not an adult.

However, if a child hits or bites or throws things when angry after the age of four-years, professional aid should be sought.

MY CHILD WAS TERMED "DESTRUCTIVE" OR "VIOLENT"

A misused adjective can lead to serious consequences. The words "destructive" and "assaultive" invariably create visions in the adult mind causing interventions appropriate for adults but not often that of children. I have heard of young children being described as "violent" by their teacher after they pushed a chair, an action that is better termed "babyish." The same could be said when a child throws an object and damages a wall or, when angry at losing a video game, the PlayStation or tablet itself. Such impulsive actions of children do not deserve the charged rhetoric applied to adult behavior.

Words have significant power. I am cautious using words in my reports, knowing that some professional terms, even those which are widely used, can be misunderstood and lead to unwise decisions. Thus, even when accurate, I did not use the term, "Elements of a Borderline Psychotic Psychostructural Organization," fearing that the person would be considered *psychotic* or *borderline psychotic* though the term means having weakness of one or more basic psychological capacities, those governing control of behavior, mood or another, because of faulty early developmental experiences. Being psychotic or borderline psychotic are vastly different matters.

How should a parent react when their child's behavior is described with such terms by their teacher? By seeking an accurate picture of what happened. "What exactly did they do?" the parent should ask, and the answer might surprise you. Sometimes it surprised even me.

One teenager, who used a stolen credit card, snuck out at night, and lied continually, caused me to consider them as having psychopathic tendencies. But after knowing them better, I came to consider the child as being enormously talented and more thoughtful about their behavior than I earlier considered.

Childhood is a time of change, struggle, and growth. Describing those events using adjectives appropriate for adults is rarely accurate and can lead to an inappropriate suggested remedy.

MY CHILD IS BOSSY AND DOESN'T PLAY WELL WITH OTHERS

Young children believe that the world revolves about them, an attitude which extends to their play. Thus, a toddler must be educated this isn't so. That they'll be liked and have more friends and more fun if they share toys and listen to others. Providing this advice won't immediately change their behavior any more than suggesting improved behavior does for an adult. You're planting seeds which, after repetitions, will germinate into their more cooperative behavior.

Having said this, some children are naturally assertive and independent which are good traits for adult living. When appropriate, children must be taught this too, and that other children can change. The child who hurt your feelings by saying a hurtful word one day may be your best friend the next day, that they did so because they were upset and now sorry how they acted.

Leaving the family to enter the larger world is a scary step for toddlers. Adults are huge, new sights and sounds abound, and they could not survive these without the loving support of their parents.

Some children are naturally loners and this is normal too. Some adults have many friends, some have one friend, and for some their only friend is their spouse. All being members of the normal continuum making up the adult personality

MY CHILD DOESN'T PAY ATTENTION IN SCHOOL

All children hunger to learn, a desire springing from the innate "effectance motivation," the good feeling experienced when one fully uses their abilities.

Thus, when a child is inattentive in school something serious keeps them from doing so. Either they are hungry, tired, physically ill, or unable to do so for an emotional reason that makes good sense to them but would seem illogical to an adult, perhaps not wanting to be bossed around.

When confronting this situation, schools and popular columnists often recommend behavior modification (reward/punishment) techniques, which seems plausible. Would anyone, whether child or adult, continue an activity for which they are punished? *Not* if they had complete control of their behavior, which they don't since the unconscious is powerful.

Behavior modification methods do work in certain locations and with select populations: in tightly controlled places like prisons, except with emotionally disturbed inmates; and with those having limited intellectual ability since it so simplifies the environment that they can function better. Of interest is that behavior modification techniques will work with dogs but not cats.

Here, the critical parental task is to determine what is making their child so unhappy that they are unable to fully use their abilities. Which is not easy since questioning a child is usually fruitless unless the distress is simple such as when caused by a classmate's hurtful comment. But incidents like these don't affect learning. Long term unhappiness does, so determining its source may require professional help.

MY CHILD TREATS THEIR PARENT(S) BADLY

Contrary to popular belief, children are reasonable, want to be liked, and will ordinarily treat others well. If not, something is keeping them from doing so, which are the same things that can affect adults: temporary conditions of hunger, illness, tiredness, or distress.

A persisting problem indicates the presence of long-term unhappiness about something, which can be anything. With an adult it might be a workplace condition. With a child, for whom school is their workplace, it can be a troublesome classmate or unsupportive teacher. During both, a situation at home might result, causing such unwanted behavior as cursing, not flushing the toilet, spilling milk, or another defiant behavior.

Educating the child is a critical first step: speaking to them slowly, using simple language, that their behavior indicates their unhappiness which their parent can't remedy unless they tell what it is. Some causes are easily determined such as when an anticipated outing is cancelled or promise broken. But often the cause is unconscious and not accessible to the child. Then a professional consultant must investigate to determine its nature.

One mother asked her twelve-year-old, angry step-son how he liked her new haircut. "It makes you look like a boy," he answered. She should have known better.

Cursing is another way that children (and adults) express angry feelings. While not easy to eliminate, a first step is to speak to the child as follows. "Though grownups do curse when they're angry, it's babyish and not a grown-up thing to do. You're smart and instead of cursing it would be better to tell me what's bothering you so I can help."

Speaking like this plants seeds of reason which, over time, will germinate into a child's more mature behavior.

MY CHILD SPOKE OF KILLING THEMSELVES OR ANOTHER

That a child's usage of words can be incorrect is not widely known. When angry, a young child may say they want to kill their parent without meaning this or even understanding what it means. One policeman became distraught when his son said this though the child simply meant they were angry. Just as a young child playing with their doll does not truly believe it is living though asserting this and relating to it as if it were.

Yet such statements do indicate a heightened level of distress that must be addressed. Thus, with a young child, the parent might say, "When you talk like that it sounds like you're really angry but not telling me what you're angry about. You must tell me this so I can help you."

The child may not know what their angry feelings stem from but this explanation gives them hope since their distress is being addressed by a powerful person (their parent) and they were given their assurance that it can be relieved. Moreover, statements like this begin their education that angry feelings are best relieved by talk rather than acting out. Which is an important lesson that even adults don't always act upon.

While suicide is rare among children it does happen, then often being termed "an accident." Children can be deeply depressed; one six-year-old boy, though not suicidal, told me, "I need a new family."

Contrary to popular belief, though almost everyone thinks of suicide or homicide at some point in their life, its incidence is relatively rare. Common statements are "I'd like to murder them" or "I feel like killing myself." What determines either possibility is: (1) there is true suicidal or homicidal intent; (2) the person possesses the means of causing death, a gun or pills or other technique; (3) the person's degree of self-control; (4) and, to a lesser degree, the presence or absence of a support system.,

Yet all such statements should be professionally evaluated. Usually when asked, the child will admit to not being serious but having been angry. A danger is inaccurate assessment at an Emergency Room leading to hospitalization which can have a devastating impact on a youth's development. While hospitalization is considered by some doctors to be the safest option, it is not always the best.

MY CHILD HAS AN ODD EATING PATTERN

Children are individual, having food preferences just as do adults. Unless suffering from a medical condition, they will usually eat like their parents, becoming accustomed to their cuisine.

But eating is also a social activity and can reflect emotional needs and indicate distress. A child rejecting a particular meal, or an entire meal like not eating breakfast, may be trying to communicate their distress in this way, or simply be identifying with a friend who also ignores breakfast. Unless their pediatrician is concerned, it's best not to interfere while educating the child about choosing healthy foods.

MY CHILD IS DEFIANT

The most common parenting complaint is what is professionally termed *Oppositional-Defiant Disorder*: when a child ignores the reasonable requests of a parent or teacher and continually behaves in a difficult manner. Refusing to get dressed for school, eating exceptionally slowly when speed is required, slamming the door, kicking the wall, running from the classroom, even blackening the toilet seat with shoe polish as one child did. Such behaviors cause the most reasonable adult to puzzle over,

An unhappy child does not always speak with their parents about it since their distress may arise from an unconscious cause which the child has no knowledge of. Instead, they behave in a manner that is certain to gain the adult's attention and indicate their need for help. Much like babies and toddlers cry when they are distressed. Recognizing this, the parent must figure out "why" while educating the child how to best cope with these frustrations in the future.

A good parental intervention is to speak as follows: "You're a great boy/girl so if you're acting like this you *must be* unhappy about something and may not know what it is. So let's investigate like a detective does, figuring out when you began feeling upset, what was happening or you were thinking of then. This is the best way to change the situation."

Depending on the child's age they may not be able to accomplish this but your intervention plants "seeds" that can germinate into their more mature behavior. Which takes time so patience is required and, as I frequently stress, providing the needed "good-enough" parenting is not easy.

If despite your encouragement their defiant behavior/distress continues, professional aid should be sought. A competent clinician should, during the first consultation session when parent(s) and child are interviewed individually, clearly explain without using professional jargon what is going on. If they do not, another clinician should be sought.

MY CHILD READS POORLY

Children reading below grade level are a large percentage of students in many public schools but being granted high school diplomas. Which, despite wide parental furor, should not be done.

The best way to prevent this is for parents to read to their toddlers at three years of age or earlier while running their finger along the book's line as they read. As the child approaches four or five, they should ask their child to help them read which, hesitantly, the child should be able to do. This is because the human mind has the genetically ingrained ability to decode (induct) the technique of reading, just as it does the grammar of whatever country into which they were born. This causes a person born in Germany to become fluent in German and a person born in Spain to grow up speaking Spanish. *Not* by memorizing all possible combinations of words which is impossible. Still, this parent technique won't be effective with all children since reading depends on intellectual and emotional factors too.

The Intelligence Quotient (IQ) is the score earned on a test designed to measure intelligence, the attempt to create this beginning in the nineteenth-century by Sir Francis Galton. Reliable intelligence testing, a test producing accurate consistent results, began in early twentieth-century France when the government asked a researcher, Alfred Binet, to develop a test to determine which children would have difficulty in school. This test, the 1908 Binet-Simon Intelligence Scale, was adapted for use in America by a Stanford University professor and named the

Stanford-Binet Intelligence Scale. An updated version of this test developed by David Wechsler for adults and children (Wechsler Adult Intelligence Scale; Wechsler Intelligence Scale for Children; Wechsler Preschool and Primary Scale of Intelligence) are considered among the best current psychology tests and widely used today.

Human intelligence is influenced by inherited and environmental factors with ninety-five percent of people having an IQ between seventy and one-hundred-thirty on the IQ scale. Those at the higher level will learn to read easily while others at the lower level will struggle with this task. But emotional factors affect all behavior and are critical too.

An unhappy child typically communicates their distress by behaving in a difficult manner and reading won't escape this. Being an activity desired by parents, this child may resist them by resisting it, either actively or by pretending inability to read. The unconscious is powerful.

Another factor may explain why some very smart children, who are good readers, so dislike it that they never read for enjoyment. I don't believe this topic has been researched, my explanation being that this resistance derives from the nature of reading itself. Being an immersive activity during which self-control is reduced, it would tend to be resisted by youth who are struggling to control their emotions because of underlying psychological issues.

MY CHILD MUST COPE WITH THEIR PHYSICAL DISABILITY

While a college student I read in a textbook about a disabled teenage girl who feared how her life would turn out. The book, *Lives In Progress,* so moved me that, decades later, I asked for one of my novels to be titled *Lies In Progress* though none of its characters were physically disabled.

Being different from peers is difficult for an adult and worse for a child who has less control over their social environment. And children can be cruel, sometimes making hurtful comments to express submerged anger toward their parents or teachers. Adopting as substitute safe target a "different" peer since a child who feels inadequate is unlikely to retaliate.

Coping behavior is how a person tolerates significant life change without experiencing crippling anxiety or depression. This can involve the psychological defense of denying the disability or intellectualizing it as by not wearing a needed brace. While these can reduce distress, they do so by reducing the ability to function optimally and cooperating with needed medical treatment.

Some parents also use denial as a coping mechanism, denying feeling distressed though feeling numb when first learning their child's diagnosis. Other parents may minimize the deformity to protect themselves from overwhelming stress. Being unable to admit to an obvious deformity reflects a distortion of reality, indicating that the person possesses inadequate psychological resources to cope with the threat and causing interference with treatment.

Studies have shown that it can be difficult for a mother to describe their child's reaction as being different from their own. Both feel threatened with one mother saying, "I didn't think it would happen to us." A child's strength to cope with their disability comes from their parents and helps their ability to cope at school.

The younger the child the less they can understand painful or uncomfortable treatments, sometimes believing it is punishment for their misdeeds. Parental feelings may be displaced onto others, blaming the school for allegedly not being sufficiently helpful rather than the critically needed doctor.

Older children can cope better with a newly discovered disability, having greater capacity for intellectual understanding and greater sense of their body. Difficulties in coping derive from: denying the threat of the deformity or the deformity itself; and lack of support from their parents which can be exacerbated by marital conflict.

To summarize, children can tolerate far more than is generally realized if given the proper support.

MY CHILD HAS ODD PHYSICAL GESTURES

Being individuals, both children and adults may have nervous gestures. With some it could be tapping their fingers while with others it could be adjusting their eyeglasses.

When in my twenties, I stood watching a military parade with a friend from childhood I hadn't seen for years. When I blew my nose he remarked, "That's what I remember about you. You were always blowing your nose." I wasn't aware of this as being a habit until his remark and am still unsure why it happens, sometimes frequently and other times rarely. It likely began as a child, being a behavior that no longer has meaning for me except as a reminder of who I had been.

Some childhood behaviors have diagnostic terms. Trichotillomania, also called the hair-pulling disorder or compulsive hair pulling, is the pulling out of one's hair on the head or about the eyes. Like biting nails, picking on skin, and tic disorders such as Tourette syndrome, all reflect distress caused by anxiety or depression.

These behaviors have an obsessive-compulsive component which is the mind's natural mechanism for reducing anxiety, an obsession being a recurring thought and a compulsion being a recurring behavior.

The best treatment for these behaviors is individual psychotherapy, which for young children is play therapy and need not last long. I have seen severe tic behavior largely disappear after several months of treatment. There is a logic to all mental health symptoms. They indicate distress and their disappearance reveals that the anxiety and depression causing it has gone, just as a bodily fever leaves once the infection causing it is absent. As does depression, which is the *depressing* of feelings from the sense of having a significant problem.

HOW CHILDREN APPROACH A RELATIVE'S DEATH

Though death is inevitable, for children it is an abstraction they have difficulty understanding depending on their age.

Preschool children view death as temporary, believing that the deceased is able to speak with them from the cloud on which they live. Older children, from about six-years to eight-years, may personify death as a frightening ghost-like form that can pursue them. Fearing it, they often believe that it happens only to the old and those who cannot run fast enough. At about nine-years-of-age they begin to understand that death is natural, irreversible, and inevitable though this concept doesn't consolidate until well into adolescence. Younger teenagers intellectualize death to protect themselves from realizing its emotional impact.

A critical adolescent task is to separate emotionally from their family, developing a separate sense of identity and place in the world. The death of someone close increases their feeling of vulnerability and undermines the sense of omnipotence associated with adolescence. Thus, teenagers who lose a friend through death often turn to peers for support rather than their family. Being unable to tolerate the emotions involved in turning back to their family just when they are beginning to separate.

Experiencing the reality of death at adolescence provokes great anxiety since it raises awareness of the fragility of life and of one's inevitable death.

PART 2 - THE TEENAGE YEARS

MY TEENAGER'S GRADES DROPPED

During the teenage years new developmental tasks arise: the child must separate more greatly from their parents; they must decide educational and vocational goals; and they explore dating as powerful sexual feelings emerge. These changes normally occur unless earlier life issues exist. Those comprising the basic ego capacities of thinking and behavior, the sense of who one is (one's "sense of self") and others. Then symptoms arise, a symptom being an indicator that something is wrong. This may be the increase of an earlier one like being defiant or a new one which can be just about anything: nightmares, anorexia, suicidal ideation, trying to self-medicate distress with alcohol or drugs and, almost always, poorer school grades since it is hard to concentrate when one is unhappy.

Yet despite being unhappy, some youth *can* separate their emotional and intellectual lives and maintain good grades but most cannot. Thus, failing school grades almost always indicate increased distress. During my initial evaluation of a child I speak first with their parent(s) alone. When they complain of their child's falling grades my next question is, "In what school year did your child do best?" Their usual reply is the year before entering adolescence.

With skillful psychotherapy, a teenager's underlying issues will be healed and their grades will naturally improve. A child wants to fully use their intellectual ability since doing so gains the positive feeling of what psychologists term *effectance motivation.* Such statements as, "I don't care" or "School isn't important" are designed to conceal the child's distress and buttress their lagging self-esteem.

MY TEENAGER'S FRIENDS GET THEM INTO TROUBLE

A critical task for adolescents is to separate appropriately from their parents and engage in the larger world with peers. To foster this and depict their new identity, teenagers may adopt mannerisms of speech and dress. Despite this, the major identity of almost all teenagers is with their family.

These essential changes are gradual and usually proceed well if the earlier psychological development was healthy. But because adolescence is a time of stress, earlier life problems may now increase or change. If a teenager lacks a secure sense of who they are or *sense of self,* " they may adopt a false identity since there is little worse than not knowing who one is. Thus, a boy (or girl) may adopt a pseudo-macho facade, a pretense of toughness to conceal their vulnerability. Lacking this secure sense of self, they may also team with an undesirable crowd causing unfortunate results: use of illegal substances or their sale; theft or assault; or behavior which may seem harmless to them but can have grave legal consequences.

One teenager's "shopping" consisted of shoplifting at the mall with her friend. As they approached the exit carrying bags filled with stolen goods, a young guard ran before them and stood by the exit. The girls' hearts sank but, as they approached the door, he held it open and said pleasantly, "Good afternoon, ladies." As the teens collapsed in their car, they decided this would be their last "shopping" event. Had they been caught and being of age, a life-altering felony charge might have followed of which they were unaware.

Teenagers may place themselves in other dangers: jumping into a lake from a height on a dare; or going to an isolated area with a stranger. Adolescence is a period of cognitive immaturity which the behavior sometimes reflects. The adult personality takes many years to form, it then having both strengths and weaknesses. Minimal problems may heal on their own but those that interfere with functioning require professional treatment.

MY TEENAGER'S LOVE INTEREST IS BAD NEWS

Adolescence is a time of personal exploration, of learning who one is, what one wants to do vocationally, where they ultimately want to live, and the love interest they are most congenial with. And, just as a youth often changes their mind about choice of occupation, so may their love experiences with comical (to an adult) or tragic results.

One fourteen-year-old boy was told by his girlfriend she was dumping him. "Okay, but we were supposed to see a movie this Friday night. Can you dump me after?" he asked. She agreed and dumped him after the movie.

Danger threatens from a teenager's involvement with a lover with personality issues of an abusive, drug-using, or criminal nature. While a healthy teenager will quickly end this relationship, those with prior difficulties may not. Then parents find themselves battling for what could be their child's life. While publicized stories of kidnap and murder by teenagers and criminal adults are rare it does happen. But family tension is common and difficult to reduce since these teenager's goals differ from their parents'. Recognizing the potential harm of their child's love interest, the parents want it to end, which is not a simple matter for their child.

For their child, the relationship is *their existence,* a conclusion mandated by short-sightedness and they lacking worldly experience. Thus, the initial parent goal must be calm discussion during which the relationship is considered objectively. Accepting that their child's search for a mate is normal but itemizing aspects of concern: physical marks on the body; increased isolation from friends and family; and lowered interest in schoolwork. Inviting the love-interest to a family meal might illustrate these points and gain information about him. If the child is intractable, professional advice should be sought to enable their development along a healthier path.

In cases involving potential danger, a referral to the Family Court using a PINS (Person In Need Of Supervision) petition may be needed. Here, the child is assigned a probation officer and an agreement governing their behavior is signed. If adhered to, the case is dismissed after several months. But if not, the child appears before a judge with wide-ranging power including their placement outside the home. Some youth, having psychological difficulty separating from their family, act out to effect this, feeling the need to be *forced* from their family. Which is undesirable since mere physical separation from the family is not identical to its healthy psychological separation and full autonomy.

MY TEENAGER USES ALCOHOL OR DRUGS

The function of all alcohol and drug use is simply to feel better. This, though significant life changes are only made by struggling with life issues and not using drugs. Thus, addiction is basically a psychological not biological issue though stopping many drugs can arouse pain and effect health. Terming it *biological* makes psychological difficulties more acceptable to many and is widely used.

Substance abuse usually begins during adolescence though it can start earlier or later. Its cause is distress, that felt by youth who fail at the critical adolescent tasks of achieving appropriate independence from parents, gaining intimacy through dating, and working toward a realistic vocational goal. Growing up in a family where substance abuse exists can be a factor but it is not the greatest one. Some youth, having early learned the harm of alcohol and drugs, will never touch them.

There is a difference between experimenting with these substances and being addicted to them. Addiction is defined as when a person's life revolves about obtaining and using them, and the interventions for this and their recreational use are different.

For occasional recreational use or experimentation, parental intervention, education, and possible outpatient psychotherapy will suffice. However with addiction, inpatient treatment may be needed and, if not addressed early, can be lengthy. Some teenagers require multiple inpatient courses of treatment before kicking the habit, causing great pain for the family through frequent lying and theft along the way.

Treatment should not be avoided by parents from feelings of guilt. Babies don't come with instructions and all parents try to do their best for their children.

MY TEENAGER IS CLUELESS ABOUT THEIR FUTURE

The choice of vocation is a critical task for teenagers, though one that need not be permanent since its change during adulthood is common. But a youth should have some idea of what they will want to do. Having a realistic goal, unlike the athletically untalented boy who hopes for a professional sports career and nothing else.

One question that I ask of every child during their mental health evaluation is the work they would like to do when an adult. Which, for a five-year-old, is often what their parent(s) does. The goal of this question is to determine if the child has an adequate *sense of self* or, as psychologists term it, sense of who they are. A child that says they don't know what they want to do tells you something important.

Similarly, a teenager lacking a realistic vocational goal will have difficulties once the structure of high school is absent. But this can happen later too. One youth did well throughout college and internship but, after graduation, sat at home having no future plan. With my encouragement, they took a sales job at a local department store until deciding.

For these youth vocational testing, which some schools offer, is a good first step. The long used Strong-Campbell Interest Inventory compares the subject's interests with those of successful people in many vocations. If similar, these vocations would be wise to consider though similarity doesn't guarantee success which demands motivation and talent too.

If this fails, psychotherapy should be considered to heal the difficulties that prevent the youth from succeeding with the adult responsibilities they will soon face.

MY TEENAGER ISOLATES THEMSELVES/STAYS IN THEIR ROOM

A youth who isolates themselves is being self-protective, trying to avoid anxiety by eliminating situations that could create it which, for some, can be any social interaction.

While people have varying degrees of social self-sufficiency, some adults having many friends while others have few or their only friend being their spouse, there is no normal number of friends. Having one friend and having many are both "normal."

Yet because some human contact is needed by all, its complete avoidance indicates their unconscious belief that interacting with others is worse than the pain of isolation. When present, psychotherapy is needed to resolve this conflict.

Video-game play is a different matter. It is a heavily obsessive-compulsive activity, an obsession being a repeated thought and a compulsion being a repeated physical activity. Both are the mind's natural means of reducing anxiety, and sometimes to avoid a "dangerous" thought from fear that it will be acted out. Despite its association with mental illness, obsessive-compulsive behavior is healthy and used by all including greatly successful people, it being diagnosable, a *symptom*, only if interfering with normal functioning.

Video-game play is healthy and associated with improved visual-motor coordination. But if played excessively to avoid normal teenage struggles, it indicates painful anxiety for which professional treatment is needed.

PART 3 - WHEN YOUR CHILD REACHES ADULTHOOD

IF EMOTIONAL PROBLEMS PERSIST

The death or severe disability of their child are the only things more painful to parents than their child's inability to perform adult responsibilities, to be economically and socially independent. And, sadly, there is no quick cure since this reflects long-term psychological difficulties which cannot be quickly healed, as Freud lamented long ago.

Possessing the maturely developed ego capacities that control behavior, thinking, and more are critical to adult functioning. Remedying their deficiencies can only be done through individual psychotherapy, gradually over time, which is why it is best that treatment begin when problems are first noticed.

The parents' task is to foster their child's hope that change is possible, stating they recognize their unhappiness and will always be there for them. If the child is attending school, absent an emergency, it is important they remain a student since study provides the needed structure and social role for one their age. The school they attend, whether college or trade school, is irrelevant. I have known youth in their early twenties who earn far above median income after graduation from trade school. One college graduate, realizing that he hated his initial goal of teaching, entered his father's trade of plumber, soon becoming so skilled that he was offered a management job on huge projects.

Full adult maturity is now considered unachieved until the mid-twenties so earlier mistakes are to be expected. An important parent task is to try to keep such errors from escalating into such potentially life altering events as legal involvement.

IF DRUG/ALCOHOL PROBLEMS PERSIST

Alcohol or drug abuse can devastate personal and family lives. Physical altercation, theft, and police involvement may occur, creating enormous stress for all with no easy solution.

Ending substance abuse is impossible without ending its use. Which is considered impossible by many addicts since its use enables them to feel better while its avoidance causes great pain. The first steps in treating addiction is to diagnose and confront it, that the patient be educated on the drug's effects, and that the addiction be halted and a support system established. Only then can the person's maladaptive attempt to compensate for psychological deficits be remedied.

Because pathological narcissism is characteristic of addicts, most don't realize their problem with drugs until they have no other choice besides ending up dead or in jail. This despite the warnings of others since addicts live to use drugs and use them to live. But stopping drug use is only one part of the long, complex recovery process since addiction often causes serious disruptions of health, work, and family.

The chronic nature of addiction means that relapse, the return to drug use after attempting to stop, should be viewed as part of the process, like a dieting person will occasionally gorge on sweets. Which does not mean that treatment has failed, only that it must be resumed, modified, or another treatment method tried.

For some, relapse is dangerous since using as much of the drug as before quitting can cause overdose since the body is no longer adapted to the previous level of drug exposure.

When treating addiction to prescription pain relievers or a drug like heroin, medication is often combined with counseling. Medication is also used to help people detoxify from drugs though detoxification is not the same as treatment or enough to assure recovery. Detoxification without treatment generally leads to resumption of drug use. Common medications to treat opioid addiction and withdrawal are Methadone, Buprenorphine, and Lofexidine.

Withdrawal symptoms can include difficulty relaxing or sleeping, or anxiety and depression. Preventing relapse is helped by avoiding the stress cues linked to the drug use such as places, people, moods, and contact with drugs,

For some, continuing involvement with Alcoholics Anonymous (AA) or Narcotics Anonymous (NA) is the answer. These world-wide organizations are abstinence-based, spiritually inclined but non-denominational, and stress anonymity. The only requirement to attend meetings is "a desire to stop using." Membership is free and there are no dues or fees.

Regular meetings are basic to the fellowship and held in church meeting rooms, libraries, community centers, or anywhere that can accommodate a meeting. Members who regularly attend the same meeting often establish a recovery network to provide a reliable routine of support. Here, there are "clean-time anniversaries" during which individuals announce their feat, receiving the group's celebration with their sponsor giving them a keepsake medallion.

The eminent eighteenth-century poet, William Blake, wrote, "The road of excess leads to the palace of wisdom,' and the noted twentieth-century psychiatrist, Harry Stack Sullivan, wrote, "We are all more human than anything else." There is only one simple prescription to the complex problem of treating addiction: whatever works!

IF YOUR CHILD IS DIVORCED

No matter how disastrous the marriage was, divorce unsettles one's life. Resembling more the demolition of a building than it's renovation and worse when children are involved.

The fear of losing permanent contact with grandchildren and (possibly) beloved in-laws is increased by the frequent Wild West atmosphere of the Family Court where, literally, anything goes and the most unexpected can happen. One long divorced woman, being sued by her ex over a transaction involving less money than his lawyer charged to prosecute the case, was so vituperous that she left court in handcuffs facing criminal and civil charges. During another Family Court hearing the judge ordered the courtroom cleared and the parent removed to the local psychiatric hospital. In another case, a mother was jailed for abusing her daughter. Upon her release, she petitioned the court that her daughter, who had been placed in foster care, be returned home. Which the judge ordered, against the advice of Child Protective Services and the child's legal guardian. The girl was murdered by her mother.

Sadly, lying is common in Family Court as is its failure to crack down on manipulative parents. My advice for those entering any courtroom is to hire the most skillful lawyer. A good lawyer's fee is small change compared to the financial and legal damage that a poor lawyer can cause.

Rather than enduring seemingly endless legal conflict, many couples enter divorce mediation during which a fair agreement is created before entering the courtroom. Though being best, this is not often followed since the heightened emotions engendered by divorce do encourage logical behavior.

My experience has taught me that older children usually know the state of their parents' marriage, sometimes welcoming its dissolution and relief from conflict that follows. But it is critical that children be told they are loved by both parents and contact with both will continue; that their lives will go on as usual, and to leave the adult matter of divorce to their parents while they cope with the problems appropriate to their age. And those divorcing need support too since the value of parents is being outgrown.

PART FOUR

INSIGHTS FOR BETTER FAMILY LIVING

As I never tire of saying: children don't come with instructions, and some *are* more difficult to parent. The following insights have been gained from my experiences in varied settings: private practice, medical school, clinic, and hospital. From these, my conclusions about mental health treatment and family life have broadened, as will yours upon their reading.

THE CRISIS IN CHILD MENTAL HEALTH

That there is a crisis in child mental health treatment is no longer questioned with nearly daily reports of parents being unable to gain immediate treatment for their troubled child.

This sorry state derives from three factors:

(1) The lack of public and doctor knowledge of child psychological development, information that could avoid creating difficulties and enable more effective treatment.

(2) Psychiatry's false, long-held biological/genetic bias about the origin and nature of mental health difficulties. This, rather than acknowledging the critical role played by parent-child interaction during early life when the basic ego capacities governing thinking and behavior, mood, and others develop.

(3) The emphasis on mental health treatment using psychotropic drugs, these having exaggerated benefits and potentially harmful side-effects.

All leading to delayed and ineffective treatment, unhelpful Emergency Room decisions, and excess hospitalization.

CANNABIS AND ANXIETY

Despite the current widespread marketing of cannabis for anxiety and other ills, it is a dangerous resource, as noted in the October 26, 2023 article in *The Wall Street Journal* ("The Cannabis That People Are Using for Anxiety Is Probably Making It Worse"). Still, living in a culture where rapid change is expected, it should not be surprising that many turn to the alleged benefits of drugs, legal and otherwise. This, despite awareness of drug manufacturers' tendency to exaggerate the benefit of their wares while downplaying their side-effects.

Anxiety is a treatable condition using drug-free psychotherapy, becoming pathological ("a symptom") only when experienced excessively.

It is a healthy reaction to anticipated threats to avoid harm. The danger may be internal or external, imagined or actual. Thus, a person whose parents discouraged feelings will feel threatened upon experiencing love, and with the same pain and fear as when a criminal with murderous intent approaches.

Similarly, *Panic Disorder*, which is a severe anxiety attack, is the *misinterpretation* of the normal symptoms of anxiety as a deadly medical event, and with the same bodily reactions as the medical danger it is believed to be.

The unconscious is powerful and one must respect its power. Yet, sadly, many doctors have become mere pill-pushers rather than the thoughtful assessors needed to facilitate healing.

MISSING PSYCHOTHERAPY APPOINTMENTS

A basic concept of psychotherapy treatment is that a behavior can have symbolic and often unconscious motive. Thus, a road rage reaction can indicate annoyance at another driver or anger from another situation: a workplace event, an unhappy relationship, or a lingering emotion from childhood.

Missing psychotherapy sessions without reasonable cause (illness, hazardous weather, death in the family), especially if the therapist isn't notified but left waiting, can reflect diminished interest in treatment, an indirect expression of anger toward the therapist, or excessive narcissism, the feeling that the world revolves about oneself.

The therapist then has two choices: to accept that, in their patient's current level of emotional development, they are *unable to* behave differently; or, if excessive, to end treatment.

It is not unreasonable to expect simple courtesy from all.

THE LIMITS OF ADULT PERSONALITY CHANGE THROUGH PSYCHOTHERAPY

Even with the best treatment the survivor of a serious medical condition is rarely as healthy as before their illness. Similarly, while psychotherapy can greatly improve behavior and emotional capacities, a patient will never be as well as if they had experienced healthier development during their formative years.

The later healing can never be total since early life experiences are the bedrock of the adult personality and the unconscious is powerful. But healing can occur outside therapy too, through nurturance during a loving relationship. Also by helping others while identifying with them, as can happen with health care workers and foster their emotional growth.

The degree of personality change effected through psychotherapy depends on independent factors: the talent and knowledge of the therapist; the intelligence of the patient; and the degree of early-life emotional damage that the patient endured.

But luck is a factor too, as with all activities both romantic and mundane. Ideal mates may meet through chance or not, and one may cross a street at the wrong time. Consider how our world would be changed had Winston Churchill been fatally injured after being hit by a car while crossing a New York City street in 1931. But even granted the best of fate, the question remains: how much change can psychotherapy effect? The answer is a great deal but not total.

Basic critical ego capacities develop early in life. These enable the child and later the adult to control their thinking and behavior, modulate their mood, and develop a secure sense of who they are or, as psychologists term it, their *sense of self*. But for these to optimally develop the child must experience adequate parenting, though not perfect parenting which no one experiences, and which depends on luck too. Even with the best intentions, as all parents have, they are a product of their life experiences, babies are not born with instructions, and good health services and nutrition are not available to all.

The therapist's overarching goal is to provide an equivalent of the good-enough parenting which the patient lacked during their development. Then, like a plant bending toward sunlight, the mind will re-develop in a healthy direction to heal past psychological and emotional damage.

Yet just as some plants that receive favorable nutrients fail to flourish, so too does some therapy fail. Adult mental development takes a long time and the inherently conservative, aided by the power of the unconscious, resists change.

Yet having regrets, feeling guilty for past mistakes, is part of the human experience and cannot be avoided when living a thoughtful life.

AUTISM IS VASTLY MISDIAGNOSED

That autism is vastly misdiagnosed is not widely known. A South Korea legislator once stated that thirty-five percent of the children in his nation were autistic. Sadly, this inaccuracy is typical of mental health knowledge in America. My first book, *Troubled Children/Troubled Parents: The Way Out*, the first chapter of which can be read on my website, includes my lengthy treatment of an accurately diagnosed autistic child.

Misdiagnoses are caused by the inadequate understanding of child psychological problems by school personnel and doctors.

To effectively treat an autistic child the therapist must enter *their* world, their personal protective shell against stress, which can be relinquished but only with proper treatment. The false belief that autistic children are uncommunicative is as erroneous as relating to them with behavior modification (reward-punishment) methods.

These children *do* communicate but in their way. With exception, schools do a poor job of interacting with or advising parents about their troubled children.

BE CAREFUL WHO YOU MARRY

My deceased dentist loved to make jokes and was one of the two authentic geniuses I met in my life. The other was a multi-lingual Columbia University professor whose advice for some odd reason stuck in my mind: that one needs a Mandarin speaking grandmother to learn Mandarin well.

But to return to my story. My dentist discovered a new antibiotic while a teenager, was rejected by medical schools because he was Jewish (it was *that* time in America) and became a dentist.

After graduation he was admitted to medical schools but refused, having opened a prospering Manhattan practice. Decades after his marriage to an enormously wealthy foreign heiress, their photo was on the cover of a national magazine in an article lauding *Manhattan's Power Couple* blissfully approaching retirement. A year later, after their divorce, the dentist told me that his ex-wife said the most hurtful thing she could: "I never thought your jokes were funny!"

HIGH SCHOOL ANGST - THANK YOU, MADONNA!
(Note: I've changed the student's name)

As high school reunions arrive, one wonders how the lives of fellow students turned out. Yet, decades later, I remembered the name of only one, Gene, and not favorably.

An old saying is that one forgets those who have done us favors but never forgets those who humiliated us, and I found this to be true. Throughout my life, Gene's name burned within my psyche.

During my lonely high school days he seemed a Gatsby-like figure. Handsome and popular, always nattily dressed and with his intended goal of Yale, he would have been a shoo-in for Homecoming King had my school such a celebration. I envied his friendships from within my social circle of one.

Gene spoke to me only once. As he approached, I felt proud, anticipating he would value me as a friend and share his approval of me with others, that I would gain friends and especially a girlfriend. But he just wanted to borrow money, which I lent him and he never repaid. Nor did he approach me again.

After reading of Gene's death in the school's newsletter, I sought information about his life from his *New York Times* obituary. There I learned that despite our differences during high school our later lives were similar. We had both earned doctoral degrees and wrote books but these were common for graduates of my selective high school from which eight graduates won the Nobel Prize and seven the Pulitzer Prize, more than any in America. But

I achieved something which, almost certainly, no other student had.

Many years after graduation, while stopped at a red light enroute to a TV interview in Manhattan, the limousine driver turned to me and said, "Madonna was the last person to sit where you're sitting." With this, I instantly told myself, "Gene, you bastard, I beat you!"

So, thanks to luck and Madonna, I *did* beat Gene in the long Game of Life.

WHEN THE PSYCHOTHERAPIST BECOMES A POLITICIAN OR HAS "PROBLEMS"

Therapists advocating political positions often blame the patient's unhappiness on these rather than unwise personal decisions. But here the patient is smarter than their doctor.

People know why they come to therapy. Throughout my years of practice, no patient *ever* raised a political issue. They spoke of anxiety or depression or marital/parenting/job problems but never that, not even those holding political office.

What causes this therapist error is a lack of understanding of what psychotherapy is and a refusal to acknowledge the power of the unconscious. As a psychiatrist colleague, a long-time government consultant, once remarked, "The unconscious is very powerful, and one must respect its power."

Inadequate knowledge of *developmental psychopathology* (a term devised by my doctoral advisor) and child psychological development has created other issues including gender misconceptions. Long ago, during a graduate school course at Columbia University ("Human Reproduction and Sexual Development") taught by an OB/GYN, the word "gender" was never uttered.

Some who avoid mental health treatment speak of clinicians having their own emotional problems, which has some truth. A long-age paper in the *Bulletin of the Menninger Clinic* acknowledged this ("The Sad Soul of the Psychiatrist") but added that experiencing and resolving life issues creates a more effective, intuitive clinician. Having unresolved emotional issues is, of course, another matter.

THE COST OF ADDICTION TREATMENT

The function of all drug use is to feel better, though this can only be accomplished by struggling with life issues and not drugs. The tendency to use drugs derives from family issues during early life development. Thus, addiction is basically a psychological and not biological issue though stopping many drugs can be painful and affect health.

Terming addiction "biological" makes psychological difficulties more socially acceptable and is widely used, being a marketing term favored by psychiatrists who compete for business with psychologists and others.

Some addiction doctors charge seven-hundred-dollar/session, far higher than even noted psychoanalysts charge. But therapy is a business, not a saintly endeavor. One charges what the market will bear though fee and fancy office decor are irrelevant to a doctor's healing ability.

SHADES OF DRACULA - THE MENTAL HEALTH DIAGNOSIS THAT WON'T DIE

The history of the ADHD (Attention-Deficit/Hyperactivity Disorder) diagnosis evidence how a profitable industry can develop from, essentially, nothing.

The concept of ADHD has a long history, being termed "mental restlessness" by a physician in seventeen-hundreds England and Minimal Brain Dysfunction (MBD) in early nineteen-hundreds America. A Harvard psychiatrist then remarked that any doctor using this diagnosis had a minimal brain dysfunction. ADHD is its most recent incarnation.

ADHD symptoms are *identical* to those of anxiety and depression, which exist in nearly every medical and mental health disturbance. When not related to a real worry (as about an impending medical diagnosis) it reflects weakness of the basic ego capacities governing thinking and behavior, which develop during earliest years and range from minimal to disabling, as has been long known.

To repeat the quote falsely attributed to P.T. Barnum, "There's a sucker born every minute."

THE ALLEGED HARM OF TABLET AND VIDEO GAME INVOLVEMENT

Tablet watching and video game play are not inherently bad, they being obsessive-compulsive in nature.

An obsession is a repeated thought and a compulsion is a repeated activity with both being the mind's *normal* way to reduce anxiety.

So when a child or an adult engages in this activity excessively, it is because they are troubled about something or that social contact makes them anxious.

Remedying this situation requires psychotherapy to eliminate the pain. Moreover, research has found that video games, no matter how awful their content, *don't* increase a child's aggression since children do distinguish reality from fantasy.

LEARNING TO READ

Learning to read and the love of reading begin at home.

Children have a genetically ingrained ability to learn to read and most should be able to read simple books by kindergarten. If, that is, their parents read first too and then with their toddlers, running their finger underneath the line being read.

Through this experience a child will *inductively* grasp the nature of reading, just as they naturally do the grammar of the language of whatever country they are born in. Thus, a child born in Spain learns to speak Spanish while a child born in France learns to speak French. *Not* by learning to place one word after another, which is impossible and would requre hundreds of years.

To further enhance your child's cognitive development *always,* apart from an emergency, *explain* your directive rather than saying, "Do it because I say so."

Not providing explanation depresses the development of both the capacity for abstract thinking and of intrinsic motivation, the "motivation inherent in information processing and action," the noted psychologist, Joseph McVicker Hunt, stated in his 1960s paper. Hunt's work was a major influence in creating the Head Start program.

SEX EDUCATION AND GENDER

Much present social dispute concerns the need for "evidence-based" education about sex and gender though these words have degenerated today into a feel-good marketing term.
The significant question in all education is what is based on objective research and what is simply disguised propaganda.

My only sex education class, which I earlier referred to, had only male students and is described in the first chapter of my novel, *Park West: A Novel of Love and Murder and Redemption*, which is posted on my website (www.drstanleygoldstein.com).

It was a graduate course at Columbia University, "Human Reproduction and Sexual Development," and taught by an empathetic, well-respected male OB/GYN. It must have impressed me since it is the only class whose name I still remember, along with several student questions that momentarily puzzled and surprised the teacher: "What is the function of pubic hair?" and "Does seeing your naked patients affect you?"

He described the likely genetic function of pubic hair as to provide protective cushioning; and said his patients were only concerned with their health though admitting, with a small smile, "Some vulvae are prettier than others."

Throughout the term, the word "gender" was never uttered.

WAS "ALAREE" A PRESCIENT SCI-FI STORY ABOUT MODERN LIFE

In a 1958 science fiction story by Robert Silverberg, *Alaree*, a crippled spaceship from Earth has landed for repairs on a small, previously unexplored planet. There, they encounter a small humanoid creature, Alaree, with whom they speak using a speech converter. The creature has great difficulty understanding the concept of *I* since on his planet all the creatures are *We*.

Alaree becomes close to the space travelers and watches as they work. Soon other aliens appear, all identical to Alaree. He implores the captain to take him back to Earth and the captain agrees after Alaree warns that he'll die if he remains on the planet.

On the return journey, Alaree behaves in a puzzling manner, staring into the face of each of the crew members as if trying to merge with them. Only after he suddenly dies does the captain understand why: because in his world he had been part of *We* and, when losing this identity and becoming an *I*, he could not survive.

This story aroused my thought of those who fear to reject popular but illogical concepts. Does this arise from their subconscious terror that, like Alaree, they couldn't survive as an *I*.

STUDENT VIOLENCE AGAINST TEACHERS

Student violence against teachers has increased, there being three dozen criminal battery assaults against teachers in one Nevada school district in 2023. Yet the needed remedy is known and would be applauded by teachers, parents, and students.

Youthful acting-out behavior varies in significance by age with a young child's hitting often reflecting simple immaturity and that of a teenager indicates serious developmental issues. Yet the remedy for both is the same: having a comprehensive psychological assessment to determine the problem and providing effective intervention.

But these cannot substitute for having school principals who won't tolerate uncivil behavior and make this clear; and mandating legal consequences for assault. Having sufficient security staff is critical too.

Several years ago there was public outrage after an assaulting teenager was pepper sprayed by police as they restrained him in school. Still, the benefit of this police action was that no one was hurt.

Learning and teaching cannot succeed where the safety of all isn't assured. Nor should teachers have to fear being held hostage to student rage.

PRISONS HOUSING THE MENTALLY ILL

There are a massive number of psychiatrically ill inmates in state prisons, some dying from suicide or poor medical care while awaiting trial. Yet this sorry situation should have been expected for several reasons.

(1) Many states psychiatric hospitals were closed with the savings not being placed into the promised outpatient clinics and supportive housing for the mentally ill.

(2) Lawyers and courts apparently believing it better to die psychotic or drug addicted but *in freedom* on the streets rather than be forcibly hospitalized.

(3) Most psychiatrists today acting as mere pill pushers rather than the thoughtful problem assessor and psychotherapist they had been in past decades.

THE SHAME OF AMERICA'S SCHOOLS

News stories have detailed the shocking inadequacies of public-school students. In many cities only single-digit percentages of high school seniors can achieve grade level scores on arithmetic and reading evaluation tests.

Having treated many teachers I can't help thinking that these deficiencies reflect less teacher inadequacy than that of school administrations: undemanding principals, and rules forbidding proper action against bullying and emotionally disturbed students. But parent behavior plays an important role too.

Were parents to first read to and then with their toddlers, most children would be reading simple books by kindergarten. But math is different since if earlier steps are missed, a child will continually fall behind.

I've known very smart children who had problems learning math so something may be wrong with how it's taught. Of this one angry retired math teacher had no doubt as she showed me the lengthy, incomprehensible to me method by which children are expected to solve a simple arithmetic problem.

ANXIETY AND IMPULSIVE BEHAVIOR

While anxiety is popularly considered a problem, it is essential to healthy functioning since it indicates when danger threatens. The issue arises when what is felt to be dangerous is not, and reflects the lingering effect of childhood experiences.

Having an immature psychological apparatus, many childhood conclusions are inaccurate particularly if gained within a troubled family. For example, if a child is made to conclude that expressing feelings, behaving independently, or that the world outside the family is dangerous, the adult will also hold these beliefs. The experiencing of healthier strivings then arouses anxiety.

Thus, anxiety can indicate both what is dangerous and what is safe but merely *felt* to be dangerous. The sufferer should decide which it is rather than behaving impulsively and unwisely.

ON SUICIDE

The suicide of famed, forty-seven -year-old Heather Armstrong, also known as Mommy Blogger and Dooce, aroused much publicity. While almost everyone sometime has a suicidal thought, the critical factors for its acting-out are: (1) that it is serious; (2) that the person has a realistic plan and means of carrying it out as a gun or pills; and (3) that the person lacks self-control.

Because of the biological imperative to live, suicide also usually requires that the person's thinking be addled by drugs, alcohol, or both as was reported with Armstrong.

Conceptually, suicide reflects early life experience during which the person was made to feel worthless with this belief returning when, burdened by exceptional stress, the person considers themselves unworthy of life and acts on this false notion.

Though the biological imperative to live is powerful, all consider suicide at some point in their life. While the actual incidence of suicide with its thought is like the proverbial needle in a haystack, it need always be professionally evaluated. Sadly, Emergency Room evaluations can be unsophisticated, leading to unneeded hospitalization.

Yet this often considered "safest" professional decision possesses emotional risk, the person thereafter viewing themselves "a crazy person" unlike earlier when they considered themselves merely human.

Suicide is always a tragedy and, as has long been said, a permanent solution to a temporary condition. Perhaps to increase its public understanding, psychological autopsies of prominent figures should be publicized. Irrespective of possible family embarrassment since, after all, this no longer matters to its principal character.

TODAY'S DANGEROUS IGNORANCE OF CHILD PSYCHOLOGICAL DEVELOPMENT

Many of today's social problems can be traced to ignorance of long accepted knowledge about the psychological development of children. This, and acceptance of the power of unconscious functioning over behavior too since early life experience is the bedrock of adult functioning.

Seemingly inexplicable horrendous behaviors can be explained by these. Most youth killings are intended to affect what is termed *suicide-by-cop* because of depression. Road-rage incidents being caused by unconscious feelings of worthlessness, and terrorist acts carried out by people who lack a healthy sense of identity, a *sense of self* that identifying with a terrorist group can seem to provide.

That an elementary biological fact has become a political issue reflects similar ignorance. While there are indisputably two sexes, what is considered the psychological characteristics of one is often present in the other.

Thus, a man may be the emotional parent in a family, behaving more maternal or *motherly*, in a role usually attributed to women; and a woman may be socially aggressive, exhibiting a trait that is conventionally attributed to a man. Yet both are completely normal.

THE POSSIBLE LINGERING EFFECTS OF CHILDHOOD
MEDICAL TREATMENT

A child's mind is immature and, when provided uncomfortable medical treatment, often blames their parents and doctor for their discomfort, being unable to grasp its need.

Post-Traumatic Stress Disorder (PTSD) symptoms may develop, these indicating that the mind's capacity to cope with stress has been temporarily exceeded.

Which can happen to anyone experiencing such stress whether a soldier, child, or adult. They then having nightmares, becoming overly sensitive to noise or the change of temperature, or developing another *symptom*, which is the signal that something is wrong.

THE ECONOMICS OF MARRIAGE

As a psychologist I hear all relationship parameters. Some couples share expenses with each being responsible for paying particular bills while others pool their earnings with one person handling all payments. When marital upset occurs, poor communication, reflective of unspoken marital issues, is usually the basic problem and not money.

Being a parent, of which the mother is usually the primary emotional caretaker, is a full-time job when considering their daily duties. Having to shuttle children to medical appointments and activities, deal with their illnesses and maybe that of a pet too, shop for food, cook meals and more. These, often, in addition to other employment.

Some mothers keep three calendars: one for their job meetings, one for their children's activities, and one for husband-wife events.

I've always been floored at the energy needed to simultaneously manage all these tasks and won't dispute those who regard women as the stronger sex.

TODAY'S ALLEGED LAZY YOUTH

Whether today's youth in their twenties are as hardworking as their ancestors is a current dispute. This, despite a newspaper article describing the life of a twenty-five-year-old engineer who completed high school in three-years, college in three-and-one-half-years, founded her software firm at eighteen, and now works well into the night; and another of a twenty-two-year-old who works sixty-hour-weeks for a corporation.

What it comes down to, in the opinion of this psychologist, is that while motivation is individual deriving from talent shaped by parenting, success depends on luck too.

On a personal note, I achieved my first book contract in three weeks thanks to a chance encounter while walking in a New York City park. Had this meeting not happened, neither might my career as an author.

BECOMING AN ADULT

The difference between the adult's and the child's view of life is that an adult can question it. A child cannot question if their world is good or bad because if they decide it is bad, that for whatever reason their parents are not supportive enough, they must also question their existence which depends on parental benevolence. Only an independent adult has the freedom to question its nature.

But this is not always true since I have known youngsters who decided that their parents were inadequate before entering high school. Then deciding to trust only *their* judgment and to make independent decisions.

But these youth also had an outsider, a loving relative or trusted teacher, to guide and encourage them. Lacking this, suicide or atrocious criminal acts sometimes occur, motivated by deep feelings of self-loathing or long smoldering rage. Situations that are avoidable by providing children the "good-enough" parenting from which healthy ego capacities and personality develop.

CREATIVE WORKS AND ARTIFICIAL INTELLIGENCE

When considering the generally poor state of public education, an important question is whether the average person will be able to distinguish the product of human creativity from that of artificial intelligence.

Re-reading the first chapter of a novel that I wrote decades ago, *Lies In Progress*, I remembered virtually nothing of the plot and would be unable to re-write the book today.

Creativity derives from the unconscious which closes when the production is completed. I can't conceive of artificial intelligence producing the twists in even a blog which combines professional knowledge with personal experiences.

Critics bemoan the effect of AI on the production of creative works, fearing it would be its death and reduce the financial livelihood of creators. I am less pessimistic, unable to conceive of software that is capable of truly mimicking a human mind.

Moreover, artists have always had a difficult financial time. H. Somerset Maugham, one of the most commercially successful writers of his time, wrote "...the successful books are but the successes of a season...the writer should seek his reward in the pleasure of his work and release from the burden of his thought; and, indifferent to aught else, care nothing for praise or censure, failure or success." Sage advice from a master of the craft.

Thus I advise teenagers that desire a creative career: figure how you'll support yourself first, then try it part-time before deciding.

THE BATTLE ABOUT SLEEPOVERS

Parental opinions are often split on slumber parties which were once considered a rite of passage. Having long treated children, I've gained insight into this dilemma.

What it comes down to is knowing both you and your child's comfort with sleepovers, and how well the other parents are known. Which is tricky when parents feel the need to interrogate them about such sensitive matters as the presence and personality of animals, the storage of guns, and potential allergic substances.

A parent who is concerned about real potential dangers is not, as has been sometimes derided, a *helicopter parent*. I've known of life-threatening allergic reactions that would terrify anyone and still remember as a child visiting a friend who playfully pointed a real gun at me.

Contrary to popular belief, sleepovers are not needed for a child's healthy development. Not before they're adult and it's with a potential mate, of course.

THE BENEFITS OF SOME DELUSIONS

Once, during a routine medical examination, I remarked to the physician that I never had a chronic illness and doubted that I would. "That's a good delusion. Keep it," she said. Which is true since the vagaries of genetics and fate are unpredictable.

A delusion, which is a fixed false belief, can exist in the personal and political spheres. Feeling unjustified guilt about their child's autism (which is a vastly misdiagnosed condition), a mother might falsely ascribe it to vaccination or air pollution.

Similarly, Anorexia Nervosa, which has the highest death rate of all mental health conditions, may be considered "normal" by its sufferer rather than resulting from damaging childhood experiences which can be healed through psychotherapy.

A person delusionally attributing their or their nation's problems to a minority population may feel better even if their life situation remains unimproved, as was evidenced in Nazi Germany and some nations today.

What determines if a delusion is beneficial or harmful depends on its effect: whether it enables better functioning without interfering with the rights of others, and fosters physical and psychological health.

CAN YOU GUIDE YOUR DREAMS?

Some believe they can guide their dreams but I'm not so sure. The unconscious is powerful and one must respect its power.

Elements in dreams arise from recent events like a movie viewed, or from long-ago memories. If, before falling asleep, you tell yourself that you will have a dream and remember it (as I advise patients to do), this will be more likely to happen but isn't certain.

If you don't record the dream upon awakening you likely won't remember it since, when awake, the conscious logical part of the mind takes control of mental functioning from the unconscious illogical part that creates dreams.

Nightmares, which are simply emotionally charged dreams, are typically remembered longer.

Those who are currently unreceptive to dealing with their unconscious conflicts tend not to remember their dreams, and dream remembrance also seems affected by some medications.

THE ROOSTER AT THE JOB

What creates the most discomfort on jobs is often not the work but having to cope with co-workers who act out family and childhood conflicts in the office. But not always.

A a caged rooster was once brought to my government office for a friend to take home at the end of the working day. It was stored on a hidden shelf in the ladies bathroom.

When a woman entered the bathroom and turned on the light, the rooster crowed, believing it was daybreak and behaving normally. A worker's complaint of hearing a rooster crow was explained by male workers as reflecting emotionality from it being "her time of the month."

LET ALL PRAISE THE SCHOOL NURSE

School can often distress students because of social discrimination, bullying, or when family issues overwhelm. This can cause the normal symptoms of anxiety to overwhelm: feeling restless, tense, or of impending doom; breathing rapidly (hyperventilating); sweating or trembling; feeling tired or weak; developing headache or stomach distress.

All quickly remedied in the school nurse's office who, in addition to her medical skills and counseling ability, provides juice and respite from stress.

Thus let us praise the school nurse, whose job often goes unappreciated though they are the student's defense when their parent isn't available.

SCREEN TIME AND HEALTHY CHILD DEVELOPMENT

A recent study found no relationship between a child's screen time and their language development. Which is logical since the human mind has an innate ability to induct the grammatical structure of language and why a child born in Germany comes to speak German and a child born in France comes to speak French.

Similarly, if first read to and then with by their parent(s) as a toddler, almost all children will induct (decrypt) the nature of reading and be able to read simple books by kindergarten.

Video-game play or *screen time* is an obsessive-compulsive activity, an obsession being a continually repeated thought while a compulsion is a continually repeated movement. This ego defense is one of the mind's most effective, developmentally mature ways of reducing anxiety.

So while an anxious child may tend to behave more obsessively and perhaps play video games or watch videos excessively, the actual problem is their distress with the real solution being its relief. Thus, the youth's online activity will naturally diminish when their discomfort is reduced.

Unless, of course, they are a potential video-game tournament star or talented software developer.

THOSE FRIGHTENING COVID TEENAGE SUICIDE STATISTICS

I tend to be leery of alarming statistics and particularly those concerning suicide. As a psychologist who has long treated children and teenagers, my experience is that true suicidal ideation, that possessing *all* the required diagnostic criteria of having a realistic suicide plan, suicide intent, possession of the means of suicide (as a gun or dangerous medication), and inadequate self-control, is rare.

Searching for such individuals is, as has been long stated, like searching for the proverbial needle in a haystack. I can remember only two youth who I referred for hospitalization from my office. While all such instances should be professionally evaluated, many youths are inappropriately hospitalized causing harmful development consequences.

Concerning the effect of the COVID emergency on academics. My experience is that some youth survived it without difficulty, doing as well academically as they usually do; others missed their friends but also performed as usual, except for math which seems especially hard when studied online; and others did poorly, particularly those for whom sports are important.

Though not an enviable situation, COVID's rapidly fluctuating rules seemed regarded by youth with equanimity, as if it were simply more adult craziness that they must endure and, when grown-up, will remedy.

REDUCING CRIME BY BATTLING THE UNCONSCIOUS

After recent horrendous murders (the Massachusetts mother who killed her three children; the killing and multiple injuries by a psychotic van driver in New York City; mass shootings) one would expect there be to wider belief in the power of the unconscious but this is not so. Instead, legislators restrict the power of judges to jail dangerous offenders, allowing them to prey until harming again when their danger is finally taken seriously.

I have long thought that the best way to increase public safety would be to increase public knowledge of facts that psychologists have long known. These include that the development of adequate ego capacities to control thinking and behavior occur during the first three years of life and depend on a child having experienced a good-enough (not perfect) parenting. And that substance abuse almost always begins during adolescence following the failure to achieve critical adolescent tasks (appropriately separating from parents; making realistic education and career decisions; dating), the youth then trying to feel better by self-medicating their distress with alcohol or drugs.

Would wider knowledge of these facts reduce crime? Ultimately, if healthier childhood experiences prevailed and better evaluation were used to distinguish criminal offenders who must be incarcerated to protect society from those being needlessly jailed and for whom other services should be provided.

ON WORKPLACE BONDING ACTIVITIES

Many corporate workers are uncomfortable with the so-called bonding events because of its implicit effect on promotion, the need to be *fun-enough* during them. Though never having worked in the corporate world apart from giving workshops, I can empathize with them.

At one government job, workers were asked to volunteer being locked in jail until bailed out with charity donations from friends. Being new to the community and knowing no one, I declined to participate.

But things were different at another job. There, at an idyllic private psychiatric hospital which provided free meals for staff and whose teenage patients felt so comfortable that they resisted discharge, patients were sent to their room early on Friday when staff gathered in the Director's office for their weekly cocktail party.

PARENT BEHAVIOR AND CHILDREN'S SAFETY

A basic human tendency is to consider other people as rational, disagreeable perhaps but rational nonetheless. Except for those who commit such unspeakable acts as the Utah father, Michael Haight, who killed his mother-in-law, wife, and their five children ranging in age from four-years through seventeen-years, two weeks after his wife filed for divorce. He had earlier removed guns from the house, apparently so his victims couldn't defend against his planned attack.

Two-years before his oldest daughter, Macie, then fourteen, reported to the police her father's multiple assaults and the extreme abuse that she suffered making her, to quote a news article, "very afraid that he was going to keep her from breathing and kill her." Which he later did.

This raised the significant question of why nothing was done by the police. The possible answer, that the wife refused to press charges, isn't sufficient since Macie had clearly been harmed. Had an adult behaved similarly toward another adult they would have been jailed (hopefully though this is not certain during these odd times). Yet the testimony of youth even older than Macie tends not to taken as seriously as that of an adult.

Another possible answer why children aren't removed from an abusing family is the prevailing belief that children are best raised by biological parents despite harmful parental behavior. This, even where judicial decisions are required to be made "in the best interests of the child." Only rarely are parental rights abrogated and children freed for adoption. Not that foster care is always better: one news item described foster parents who not only sexually abused their two young wards but prostituted them.

Clearly, sophisticated evaluations are needed of both criminals and foster parents. And greater education of police and judges too with the hope that better decisions be made, those consistent with child safety rather than hoary philosophy.

INSTANT NEWS ANALYSES OF ARRESTED ALLEGED KILLERS

Published comments from those having earlier interactions with the alleged Idaho killer of four youth, Bryan Kohberger, are like those arising after other mass killings in which common behaviors are considered to foreshadow violence.

These, noted by past acquaintances of Mr. Kohberger, included student criticism of his harsh grading (which lessened as did his apparent teaching motivation following their protest), talking down to a fellow graduate student, and quickness of temper. All that can be said of virtually every college teaching associate. For most this is their first teaching assignment which can be frightening. Losing job motivation and easing grading when confronted with student protest are common developments.

Perhaps part of the need to quickly comment is our horror at the crime and desire to distinguish between the criminal and ourselves, to emphasize that we could *never* commit such a heinous act. Which is true for virtually all unless they be addled by drugs or alcohol.

Yet this attitude also reflects the limited public knowledge of child development, ego psychology, and especially the powerful influence of early parenting on a child's immature mind, these being when beliefs are created that become the bedrock of the adult personality.

And as I often state, the unconscious is powerful and one must respect its power.

FEAR AND HEROISM DURING CRISES

Chance can lead to death or survival as when a snowstorm enveloped Buffalo. A stranded driver, twenty-seven-year-old mechanic, Jay Withey, was rejected by ten homeowners when he knocked on their door seeking shelter. This, despite his offer of five-hundred-dollars to let him sleep on the floor of their home. Then, after leaving, he rescued others by breaking into a nearby school for refuge.

I can't imagine why the sight of Mr. Withey so frightened the homeowners that he was sent into what could have been his death. But certainly those he later rescued are glad that the homeowners did.

EXPLAINING THE PSYCHIATRICALLY HOSPITALIZED ADOLESCENT

The adolescent whose acting-out is so severe as to require treatment in a psychiatric hospital suffers from psychological damage that occurred during their second and third year of life. The normal infant-mother symbiosis and its separation didn't occur with the child failing to develop a secure sense of who they are, and *soothing introject*, the ability to comfort themselves.

These early life issues are increased during adolescence by distress at the inability to cope with critical tasks: appropriate separation from parents; exploring intimacy through dating; and creating realistic educational and vocational goals.

Revolving-door treatment cannot aid such youth. They need a secure therapeutic environment within which their defective ego capacities can redevelop, thus enabling them to function in the adult world they will soon enter.

For more disturbed youth, longer-term residential treatment is needed. Others, less disturbed, can accomplish the needed psychological changes through individual out-patient psychotherapy.

SUICIDE IN THE MILITARY

A study of suicide in the American military found that the more concurrent risk factors which were present, the greater was the risk of suicide with the greatest risk factor being the loss of an intimate relationship.

Other risk factors included: job, administrative, or legal problems; the sufferings of Post-traumatic Stress Disorder (PTSD); and having had combat experience coupled with substance abuse.

It was recommended that the Defense Department's emphasis on mental health education and support should be expanded to include spouses and intimate partners.
From *Risk Factors Explaining Military Deaths From Suicide, 2008-2017: A Latent Class Analysis*" by Scott D. Landes, Janet M. Wilmoth, Andrew S. London, and Ann T. Landes in Armed Forces & Society, January 2023, Vol 49, Number 1, pp 115-137.

THE HISTORIC PSYCHOANALYTIC MODEL OF TREATMENT AND PERSONALITY CHANGE

The historic psychoanalytic treatment model of silently listening to patients and interrupting only with an occasional interpretation is rarely useful since it lacks much of a living experience.

Nor is it helpful to offer such hoary wisdom as "all people have problems." Instead the clinician should, by providing psychological facts and instructive anecdotes, educate their patient on the complexity of life, the need to experiencing an adequate childhood to avoid emotional difficulties, and of their tendency to persist.

Unrealistic fantasy has great power to disrupt life since it can be enjoyable even when fearful, and the mind has only limited power to defend against it.

While only brief psychotherapy may be needed to help with a recent isolated life problem, the treatment of deeper discontents must be lengthy (though not interminable) since psychological limitations are long in development and the mind, being inherently conservative, resists change.

Yet the mind also contains an inherent thrust toward psychological health and life fulfillment with dreams and nightmares communicating both the unconscious awareness of the need for change and of its fear.

WHEN YOU FEAR YOU'RE GOING CRAZY

While the fear of "going crazy" is widespread, it is really a very difficult state to achieve requiring either drug/alcohol abuse or long-term overwhelming stress.

This fear contains several elements: lacking self-control; having impaired thinking; and being unable to care for oneself resulting in the need for hospitalization.

What underlies this fear for most people is the loss of self-control. This caused by the sudden realization of angry feelings or dependency needs, both of which would be lessened by hospitalization.

Yet this fear of losing control can also be caused by something innocuous, like becoming tearful by one who never does.

BULLYING UNIVERSITY PROCEDURE AND A TEENAGER'S SUICIDE

Any youth's suicide is shocking but that of Stanford University's soccer star/college senior, Katie Meyer, was particularly upsetting.

While every suicide reflects complex emotions, the action creating her precipitating stress seems particularly illogical and unwarranted. According to a November 27, 2022, article in *The Wall Street Journal,* Ms. Meyer had been accused of spilling coffee on a fellow student who had been accused of sexual assault by another student, an accusation that was considered unworthy of action by either the school or the police.

Despite this, an administrative charge was filed against Ms. Meyer by the University's Office of Community Standards. Six months later she was informed of a pending disciplinary charge that could result in "removal from the university," and her diploma being placed on hold. After replying to this e-mail that she was "shocked and distraught," she killed herself.

In hindsight, she should have informed her parents, who likely would have hired a lawyer to quash this nonsense, but great stress inhibits rational thinking. What is clear is that the 1972 Title IX civil rights law prohibiting sex-based discrimination, which was intended to protect students from harm, is now being used to bully them.

HEALING SCHIZOPHRENIA

The crippling behaviors termed *schizophrenia* have their origin in infancy and toddlerhood when the child's capacity to distinguish themself from the surrounding world fails to develop normally. This derives from faulty interaction with their parenting figure, who is usually their mother but can also be their father or another continually involved adult.

Because of this the basic perceptual abilities which include the sense of who one is or their "sense of self," the ability to distinguish reality from fantasy, and the ability to modulate mood are deficient causing later problems in functioning as adult.

Treatment, which is not simple or brief, consists of providing the supportive interpersonal experience which enables healing of this childhood psychological failure. Drugs cannot accomplish this; only human interaction can.

Incidentally, schizophrenia is often mis-diagnosed, particularly when alcohol or drug abuse is present.

PSYCHOLOGICAL IGNORANCE AND BLISS IN MODERN SOCIETY

The astounding present number of unsophisticated beliefs about behavior is caused by widespread public ignorance of psychological functioning and development. which can come from the lips of clinicians too.

Consider treatment acronyms like DBT, *Dialectical Behavior Therapy*, which I thought to be *Diabolical Behavior Therapy* when first hearing it. This and others are merely the cannibalization of the four basic treatment modes of psychoanalytically oriented psychotherapy: *Relationship*, *Replacement*, *Supportive*, and *Analytic*.

These merely indicate periods during treatment in which the therapist-patient *Relationship* is emphasized, when the *Replacement* of the patient's deficient ego capacities with more mature ones is prominent, when the Supporting of present psychological strengths is primary, and when the patient's behavior is *Analyzed* by relating present conflicts to early life experiences.

An enthralling Netflix documentary series about a Hollywood teenage burglary ring that robbed celebrities is *The Real Bling Ring*. As crazed (but clever) was their robbery planning is the celebrity culture that they hungered to join.

And regarding being *traumatized* by a scene from a book or film or comment: when one doesn't know the clinical definition of *trauma* it can be used to mean *feeling upset* or *not liking it* or having *hurt feelings*. Development as an adult requires learning to cope with such human failings as jealousy and envy and sadism, in jobs and elsewhere.

A woman once told me that her therapist said, "I love you." "Wow! That's a pretty unusual thing for a therapist to say," I responded. "Well, he didn't say *exactly* that. He said, 'You're lovable.'"

When words can mean anything and belief becomes fact, we exist in a world in which everything is OK and acceptable, or perhaps a crazy one.

ON ACHIEVING A HAPPY MARRIAGE

During my work as a psychologist I have learned of devastating marriages and divorces, with some being too improbable for a novel but lived by people who felt that attraction and not personality is what matters in a relationship. But emotional immaturity and impulsivity are key warning signs, as is a history of abusive relationships and over-dependence on parents.

Yet it takes time to know someone too. In 1930s Vienna, an unmarried American psychiatrist underwent his six-month training analysis with Sigmund Freud. Before the doctor's departure to return home, Freud said he hoped that the doctor would have the good fortune to achieve a happy marriage. "Does one need luck with all your psychological knowledge?" the doctor asked, and Freud replied, "Certainly, for only after living with someone for a long time does one really know them."

MY SATIRE ON ENSURING THAT PSYCHOTHERAPY FAILS

In addition to the therapist lacking talent and training, certain professional practices ensure that a patient's treatment will fail:

(1) Using a vague unintelligible diagnosis will cause the patient to be considered untreatable. One such as "Borderline Personality Characteristic Reflective of Post-Autistic Development" would be excellent. To increase confusion and professional acceptance, a biologic or genetic phrase can be added like "Possible malformation of the patient's adrenal medulla causing irregular production of the epinephrine and norepinephrine hormones may be influencing the patient's moods."

(2) Advising that psychological deterioration is inevitable unless many years of thrice-weekly individual treatment is obtained since this is rarely possible.

(3) Having the most disturbed patient be treated by the clinic's least experienced worker. A beginning trainee is a wise choice.

(4) Making life decisions for the patient. This will further lower their self-esteem by indicating how inadequate their doctor believes them to be.

(5) Never responding directly to a patient's question. So if asked why their symptoms exist the doctor should reply, with an air of condescension and omniscience, "Severe problems like yours take a long time to understand." This, even if the symptom has

been long understood since psychotherapy is least likely to fail when a patient receives clear explanations.

THE CHILDHOOD ORIGIN OF ANOREXIA NERVOSA

Though the psychodynamics of Anorexia Nervosa has long been understood, it remains the deadliest of mental health disorders having the highest death rate. Its origin lies in parental failure to encourage their child's independence, with the child's only possible autonomous behavior being control over what they eat.

Symptoms begin at a time of expected independence for this socially immature child who has little awareness of their feelings, with the struggle around eating substituting for the normal developmental struggle of separating appropriately from parents and entering more mature relationships.

Thus, symptoms arise when personal autonomy is required: beginning school, entering puberty, or leaving for college.

The initial treatment goal must be to restore and maintain the patient's healthy nutrition. Apart from creating critical bodily issues, starvation causes increased irritability, hyperactivity, and obsession with food.

Individual psychotherapy can help the patient resolve their dependency issues, with their low self-esteem naturally rising as normal developmental goals are achieved.

WHEN CREAIIVE CORPORATE LEADERSHIP
DETERIORATES INTO PARANOIA

A new manager's initially successful behavior can deteriorate into paranoia if their positive abilities of alertness to change and goal directedness descend into rigidity. Then, delusions of grandeur may arise which foster unrealistic projects and irrational suspicions causing scapegoating, poor morale, and high staff turnover.

The checks and balances of a conscientious corporate board can enable needed organization change while protecting the staff against the abuse of power, forcing the manager to abide by reality not fantasy and rescuing them from what Plato described as "convulsive fear and distractions."

ON TRANSFERENCE AND COUNTER-TRANSFERENCE DURING PSYCHOTHERAPY

Healing during psychotherapy occurs through the therapist-patient interaction which, ideally, is the "good-enough" parenting which the patient lacked during their development. In this process, unconsciously derived reactions of the therapist are common: forgetting an appointment, day-dreaming during the therapy sessions, or feeling bored.

Identified as *transference* on the part of the patient and *counter-transference* on the part of the therapist, they are inevitable. Though reducing the effectiveness of treatment, they are part of the human condition, occur whenever people interact, and can point the therapist toward interactions that provide better treatment.

PREVENTING IMMINENT SUICIDE

Though suicide is never an acceptable alternative to living, it can feel that way when enduring continuing unbearable anxiety and hopelessness. One might also choose suicide to communicate how intolerable their life had become.

During this struggle between life and death a relationship with a compassionate friend or psychotherapist, from whom to draw strength, can enable time for ego strength and self-esteem to recover with the powers being focused on life and not ending it.

Then freed from the self-imposed punishment of death, the person can then use their abilities to resolve important life issues.

COPING WITH WORK OR MARITAL CONFLICT THROUGH TRIANGULATION

Triangulation is the reduction of anxiety in a problematic relationship by introducing a *third* element into the situation. At work this can be a person or a corporate directive being depicted as "crazy" and in marriage a child being termed "impossible."

Though reducing anxiety, this unconscious maneuver is destructive since it doesn't resolve the problem. To accomplish this a third party, a management consultant or psychotherapist, must reframe communication so the real issues are confronted.

Yet here triangulation can also occur if the consultant identifies with the worker or the psychotherapist with the patient(s). As I never tire of repeating, the unconscious is powerful and one must respect its power.

PSYCHOGENIC ("VOODOO") DEATH

Though popularly believed a folklore belief of primitive societies, psychogenic death ("voodoo death"), a healthy person's demise solely because of their belief, has been well documented.

In these cases, people find themselves in an impossible situation. Unable to struggle, flee, or fight, with their giving-up often complemented by rejection of important nurturing figures.

During psychotherapy this can an ending of the intense emotional attachment of patient to therapist, resurrecting the childhood fear of rejection by their mother and akin to cutting the umbilical cord too soon.

This belief of inescapable death can be reversed, ending the person's deterioration by introducing a powerful figure into their life, a family member (particularly their mother) or more flexible therapist.

EARLY CHILDHOOD EXPERIENCES THAT FOSTER THE DEVELOPMENT OF ADULT EMOTIONAL PROBLEMS

A child's mind grows by borrowing aspects of themselves from their parents while weaving their unique view of the world.

While many aspects of the child's philosophy of life, their "story," are accurate, their immaturity inevitably creates errors of belief, leading to difficulties in relating to themselves and others.

If deprecated by their parents they may consider themselves worthless and unlovable, an apparently valid conclusion since their God-like parents think little of them. Healthier experiences produce feelings of confidence and optimism.

The development of an organized sense of who one is, what psychologists term the *sense of self*, begins at birth through interaction between the infant and their caretaker, who need not be a biological parent.

When only one of the children in an abusive family develops into a healthy adult, it is often because of an outsider's long-term influence, a relative or a teacher, with the child's mind having "fed" on this nourishing infusion as does an ill person's body their healing medication.

POTENTIAL PERSONALITY CHANGE FOLLOWING MILITARY COMBAT

Violence can cause a change of personality and military combat is among the most intense experiences. One personality change, called the "heart of darkness" syndrome, transforms a previously normal person into an enjoyer of killing. This exceeds the normal reactions to prolonged combat though the soldier had earlier expressed no antisocial behavior and had a close, caring relationship with their comrades. The personality changes from "normal" to "happy killer" occurred after witnessing their comrades' deaths.

This reaction to the trauma of combat is extreme. Soldiers enduring only brief combat need not make such a reality adjustment to psychologically survive, having adjusted to it with controllable fear during their potentially fatal experiences.

But continuous combat tends to produce a sense of denial, despite the close-by death of comrades, causing a blunting of feelings which can affect relationships long after military service has ended.

Three possibilities exist within the continuum of personality change after combat:

(1) None, where the ex-soldier remembers and re-experiences past events without denial, the blunting of feelings, or becoming a lover of killing.

(2) The soldier develops a warrior mentality but functions under orders, killing only for military purpose and retaining a sense of ethics.

(3) The soldier has come to love killing, they feeling invulnerable and lacking empathy for those whom they kill.

Murder and Evil

During my first job as psychologist at a psychiatric hospital, I told my psychoanalyst/supervisor my teenage patient's statement. "That's psychotic," the doctor replied. Though able to define "psychotic," until that moment I hadn't grasped the power of this condition.

Similarly, after mass murder horrors are reported, the perpetrators tend to be viewed with surprise for they *look* so normal, lacking the twisted features of horror film characters despite having the same bogus beliefs.

Columnists ask the usual question "why" and provide their usual answer "no one knows." Which is not true! While predicting violence cannot be certain, it correlates highly with several factors: failure in life; substance abuse; the ego capacities governing thinking and behavior being inadequately developed; and having a fragmented *sense of who one is*. The killer's frequent decision to suicide is considered preferable to their continued painful existence.

And though their act was horrendous, these individuals are not often considered "insane." The legal definition of insanity is determined by state statute, most usually whether a person can distinguish "right" from "wrong" and, contrary to popular belief, rarely succeeds as a defense.

But to describe these individuals as "sane" does not imply they possessed normal control over their behavior. Still, except for those possessing extreme psychological limitations, this should not influence their punishment.

There is evil in the world and some succumb to temptation. Yet even for others, the unconscious is powerful and one must respect its power.

The Real Reason For School Discipline Problems

Students misbehave for one or more of three reasons.

1. A child's ability to control their thinking and behavior depends on basic ego capacities which form within the first three years of life. Their adequate development occurs through a healthy interaction with their parents. If lacking, weakness will exist of these crucial abilities producing their later failure to function maturely.

2. Students with emotional problems will occasionally be uncooperative. Schools, with exception, are clueless about coping with such difficulties and for good reason: teachers are trained to teach in a school, not operate a therapeutic environment.

3. School principals who do not take discipline seriously, by quickly intervening against bullying or other uncivil behavior, send the implicit message that these are not serious issues. Both students and staff soon get this message with student behavior, teacher motivation, and academic achievement deteriorating.

While these issues are not easily addressed, ignoring them by choosing the false explanations of prejudice or inadequate school funding makes change impossible.

THE POLICE OFFICER, THE DOCTOR, AND THE ANNUAL MEDICAL EXAM

While apparently dissimilar, the work of the police officer and the doctor share an essential characteristic. Both must wait before intervening: the police officer for the crime and the doctor for the symptom, which may be long in development. No law or medical guideline allows personal rights to be violated regardless of potential benefit to society or the individual.

While the medical model of treatment forbids intervention until illness is apparent, a corollary principle is that illness should not be ignored. To resolve this conflict demands an uncommon level of practice, the ability to note subtlety of words, tone, and behavior within the framework of psychological knowledge.

Thus, the ritualized annual health check-up has minimal effect on critical issues since it ignores the early stages of psychological stress, from developmental issues, family, and work, that can lead to organic illness.

An ancient principal of psychosomatic medicine is that what cannot be spoken will be expressed through bodily symptom.

*THE UNCONSCIOUS FACTORS UNDERLYING SOME
LEARNING DIFFICULTIES*

Psychology has long known of the association between unconscious emotional attitudes and academic failure, or that an academic subject can be considered disagreeable because of its association with a parent's occupation.

Thus, apparent reading difficulty can result from: the refusal to submit to the order to read, feeling that it infringes on one's autonomy; the fear of losing one's *sense of self* (sense of who one is) during emotional involvement in a book; or the unconscious desire for criticism and punishment.

A child's problems with their mother, who is the most important emotional figure in their early development, can also extend to their relationship with their teacher. An overly narcissistic mother or one who considers their child defective, will hinder their child's ability to adapt to reality, particularly when speech is used to gain praise rather than to communicate.

Underachievement, the failure to learn, can also reflect hostility, it being an indirect, safe passive attack on parents and society who considers the task important.

Clearly, for some, the powerful, instinctive hunger to learn has been throttled.

OF ADULT ANXIETIES AND LINGERING CHILDHOOD FEARS

Beliefs about anxiety have a long illustrious history. Pascal, the French seventeenth-century child prodigy, mathematician, and physicist, suffered from anxiety and wrote "all of the misfortunes of men derive from one single thing which is their inability to sit still in a room." Even today anxiety is the most frequent mental health diagnosis, having as a common complaint the inability to sit still.

Yet were humans unable to experience anxiety its species could not endure since it is a critical survival mechanism: the reptilian instinct that mortal danger approaches and warning of the need to prepare. Today these dangers are rarely lethal, they referring to job or relationship difficulty.

While some fears are easily understood it is the inexplicable ones that frighten most, erupting as they do from the bedrock of personality created during childhood. During the struggles for autonomy, self-assertion, and intimacy, leaving fragments to do battle.

Once, during my successful treatment of a young child, her mother shared her own troubled childhood. After my comment that her mother "had issues," she instantly retorted, "My mother was a perfect mother," stormed from my office, and removed her daughter from treatment. A woman in her eighties, the recipient of numerous national awards, said after receiving her latest, "I wish my mother could have seen this."

Childhood-based feelings linger throughout life, being expressed in yearnings, artistic creations, self-defeating behaviors, and fears.

THE BORDERLINE PERSONALITY DISORDER CONTINUUM

Like all mental health disorders, people suffering from Borderline Personality Disorder exhibit symptoms of varying severity depending on their capacity for relationships.

Those closest to a psychotic disorder are openly angry, having given up their desire for closeness. Less severely impacted are those that vacillate between moving toward and away from others.

The next group lacks a secure *sense of self*, sense of who they are, and mold their behavior according to what others expect. The least disturbed group continually seek a symbiotic relationship with a mothering figure, having lacked a "good-enough" (though not perfect) parenting early in life.

This continuum of pathology reflects the inability to tolerate intimacy which causes a movement toward and away from others.

The diagnosis of Borderline Personality Disorder is often incorrect, particularly with those suffering substance abuse and *always* with children since its diagnosis requires an *adult* mental structure which children lack.

THE TWO CURATIVE ELEMENTS IN PSYCHOTHERAPY

Several factors comprise the healing elements of all individual psychotherapy, both the classic psychoanalytic treatment which is uncommon today and suited for few, and the frequent psychodynamic treatment.

Insight into one's behavior, though it having less effect than has been dramatized in movies since a patient may gain great insight but small change of life.

A second factor is the patient's attachment to their therapist, the therapeutic alliance, within which a more benign and thoughtful concept of themselves is adopted. During this corrective emotional experience the patient comes to view themselves and others differently, and long-held, unconscious terrors become extinguished.

EXPLAINING PSYCHOSOMATIC DISORDERS

The human organism was once an undifferentiated mass from which subsystems developed: the enzymatic (hormone) system; the nervous system; the psychological system; and the organ system.

Their boundaries are imprecise with activity in one being continuously communicated to others. Thus, a change in one that is caused by stress causes changes in others with their normally smooth integration being affected.

While stress initially arouses helpful body defenses, too great stress causes a breakdown between system boundaries, a *de-differentiation* during which energy may be discharged through violent fighting activity or running movements.

Mild anxiety is experienced as a signal of danger and can cause more efficient action or thinking. But if the anxiety is too intense, psychological means or behavior are unable to reduce it. Then, primitive psychosomatic defenses may stir up harmful bodily effects, an illness or a disability, that can persist after the anxiety disappears.

WHY NURSES LEAVE VETERAN ADMINISTRATION (VA) HOSPITALS

Research on why nurses leave Veteran Administration hospitals, by Dongjin Oh' and Keon-Hyung Lee, was reported in the October 2022 issue of *Armed Forces and Society* (pp. 760-779).

The biggest factors were emotional burnout and stress. This was caused by the sense of loss, grief, and powerlessness over the frequent deaths of patients who they had long cared for. Far more patient deaths occur after VA hospitalization than in civilian hospitals since VA patients are older with many having been exposed to harmful environments during their military service.

An excessive workload from the VA's policy of having nurses work overtime because of staff shortage reduced their ability to recover from grief. Being ordered to do time-consuming non-nursing tasks, and the lack of flexibility in work scheduling which would enable a healthy work/personal life balance were other factors.

The same could be said of nurses at other hospitals during the COVID crisis when patient workloads were high and critical medical equipment and masks were often lacking.

HOW THE INNOCENT CAN BE JUDGED GUILTY

Though the human mind tries to make sense of events efficiently it sometimes gets it wrong. In a hotel outside Boston, because of COVID the usual "room refreshening" wasn't done for short stays. Because it lacked a restaurant, I had brought snacks from home: a loaf of bread, cans of salmon, and small cups of apple sauce, placing them in the room's kitchenette's small refrigerator before leaving. Next day, wanting a snack, I found them gone and concluded the obvious: that they had been stolen. Yet nothing else was missing and an unfinished cup of tea that I made earlier was still in the refrigerator.

I phoned the desk clerk and inquired. "This'll sound crazy but I'm not psychotic. The food that I put in my refrigerator is gone. Was someone in my room?" I asked suspiciously. Feeling perturbed even after her assurance that my privacy hadn't been violated. Yet why would any thief steal only the food?

Later, noticing a small black cabinet in the living room, I opened it and discovered my missing food, only then realizing that there were *two* refrigerators in the suite, one in the kitchenette where I placed my tea after making it and the other in the living room where I placed the food.

When a hotel employee later came to fix a phone, we laughed as I described my mistaken conviction and I asked him to inform the desk clerk that my vanished food had re-appeared.

THE CRITICAL NEED FOR THE PSYCHOLOGICAL EVALUATION OF INMATES

No psychologist likes working in a prison since even those having supportive congenial colleagues contain uncomfortable characteristics: being unable to keep a personal phone within the institution and having to exit multiple locked gates before rejoining the normal world. Yet these psychologists play a critical role.

While a county chief psychologist I often evaluated inmates at the local jail. An experience which, perhaps contrary to popular belief, they valued and even enjoyed. Life in a local jail lacks the treatment and educational facilities of larger state prisons so the undivided attention of another person is not a gift to be spurned.

Moreover, comprehensive psychological testing, which includes intelligence and personality instruments, is interesting and provides exhaustive information. So much that my reports were termed "magic" though their creation reflected the lengthy psychometric research of past generations.

By helping judges make better informed decisions, my reports aided inmates. A young man who had violated parole was released when my testing found him to be intellectually limited. Another inmate, who was charming except when being pressed with questions, already had a new girlfriend, his former having left after his arrest for rape. My interview revealed that his unconscious rage toward women was motivated by childhood abuse.

Society would be safer and more just if psychological testing played a greater role in the judicial system.

WHY BATTERED WIVES REMAIN MARRIED

Why women who endure threats and assaults from their spouse remain with them seems inexplicable yet is easily understandable since, through their experiences, they have been programmed to be submissive. Enslaved by their husband through a paralyzing terror of continuous agitation, anxiety bordering on panic, and psychosomatic symptoms which create passivity and feeling hopeless. Rarely, their deeply repressed rage erupts in murder.

Studies revealed that many of these women had alcoholic fathers and married as teenagers when pregnant. Husbands drank heavily and kept their wives isolated with false accusations of infidelity. Beating them after their return home and causing the women to live in constant fear, unable to meet with supportive female friends and keep medical appointments.

Their low self-esteem, lack of safety and financial resources, and feeling shame are what causes them to stay with their battering husband.

CRIME AND POVERTY

It is not poverty that causes crime but, largely, the lack of healthy childhood experiences since these are critical to the development of the ego capacities governing control of thinking and behavior, modulation of mood, and the development of a sense of self (sense of who one is) which are essential to independent adult functioning.

This explains why some children who experienced desperate poverty become law-abiding, financially independent adults while the lives of others go awry.

Today's philosophical and political tunnel-vision largely exists because knowledge of child psychological development is lacking.

1984 REDUX OR CURRENTLY PERMITTED LANGUAGE

A robust discussion about the "sensitivity industry" on the Authors Guild Community website detailed how book publishers now take seriously criticism from even unknown online complainants. In one case, criticism of a bunny in a book aroused corporate angst though NOT from a bunny.

To these comments I added my experience of participating on a Facebook parenting group where, in response to the unsophisticated comments, I explained Borderline Personality Disorder as a developmentally derived weakness of basic ego capacities. Then being criticized for using the term "weakness" since this allegedly put people down. I thought to respond that, following this logic, tuberculosis and polio should be considered other than disabling but didn't. Responding to know-nothings is fruitless.

My tolerance for idiocy having been exceeded, I dropped out of Facebook parenting- advice groups after one group's moderator stated that anyone who henceforth used the term "breast-feeding" in place of "chest-feeding" would be expelled. I reported this incident on the Authors Guild Community website and a cleverer writer than me advised that I should have responded, "Send me your child to chest-feed."

Others contributed similarly with one writing that employees of a West Coast state mental health department were instructed that henceforth the term "insane" should be used in place of "crazy," while another posted that his friend at a Washington

D.C. facility was ordered to use the term "crazy" in place of "insane." You figure.

All this left me puzzled. I have long believed that, when considering all their responsibilities (home, child-care, job, ill pet, etc.) it is fortunate that women have babies since they *must be* the stronger sex. But will I be pilloried for saying this?

HELPING A CHILD WITH A SEVERE ILLNESS

Being seriously ill as an adult inevitably arouses terror, an experience that is infinitely worse for a child since their understanding lacks mature insight. They may even perceive their parents as deliberately taking them to doctors who cause them discomfort and pain. Which is unavoidable for sufferers of cancer or convulsive disorders even when the prognosis is favorable. The child feels friendless, having none who can understand but their stuffed animal friend who mutely observes.

Young children consider their stuffed animals to be friends no different from living friends with whom adults share their secrets. Children talk to these "friends," play with them, and sometimes hurt them which, like parents, they lovingly forgive.

Explaining the child's medical situation, using simple terms and their "friend" as intermediary, can relieve their trauma and isolation and give hope.

Parental success in coping with their child's lingering medical illness can derive from the quality of their interactions with their child's doctors. Some doctors speak vaguely regarding diagnosis and prognosis but others describe the illness realistically. Focusing on possible research breakthroughs and the parents' hopes during remissions when the child lives comfortably at home.

Yet family sadness is inevitable too since, until the child's diagnosis, they were considered normal and happy rather than chronically ill and suffering.

LIVING WITH A TYRANNICAL BOSS

What a worker can tolerate in a boss' behavior is individual. One woman calmly worked for several years beside her erratic yelling boss in the entertainment industry. The survivor of a difficult childhood, she had lived in her car until being helped by a concerned college teacher who let her live with her until graduating from college. Upon quitting her job, the young woman was asked to train her replacement to tolerate the screaming boss.

It's time to leave a job when psychosomatic symptoms such as neck pain begin. I've often said that I may not have been too smart about some of the jobs I took but knew exactly when to leave, which is when the boss wants you to stay. I've learned that a manager has a certain "shelf life," initially being viewed as the organization's savior but, once it functions well, becoming considered part of lingering problems.

Still, as my (now deceased) graduate school advisor wrote after receiving my letter of woe, "Think of the job as being a chapter in your memoir." Sound advice for all to follow.

PARENTAL RELUCTANCE TO CONFRONT THEIR CHILD'S EMOTIONAL PROBLEMS

A mother brought her child to my office. While speaking with her alone, I referred to her son's "emotional problems." "My child does not have emotional problems," the mother insisted and stormed from my office. Had I been given the chance I might have asked, "Then why are you here?" but already knew the answer: to gain reassurance that, despite having long observed her child's bizarre behavior, he was completely healthy.

This illogic, when a parent's conviction clashes with reality, is understandable. It indicates the parent's feeling of shame based on their belief that they failed as a parent. Which is undeserved since a child has individual needs, is not born with instructions, and abruptly arrives on *their* schedule into an unselected family. Once parents gain help for their troubled child, they have no reason to feel guilt, which is counter-productive to successful treatment.

But *not* seeking treatment for a troubled child, especially when it leads to harm, is inexcusable.

SHOOTING ATROCITIES AND POLITICIAN RESPONSE

While guns should certainly be kept from children and the mentally disturbed, behaving simplistically accomplishes little. Which politicians tend to do following a fearsome crime.

The cause of many shooting atrocities is mental illness with virtually all deriving from the inadequacies of childhood when the basic ego capacities governing control of thinking and behavior form. Yet no politician speaks this and likely few know it since child development knowledge is minimal even for doctors.

What many seem to fear even more greatly than guns is awareness of the fearsome power of the unconscious. Perhaps a gun symbolizing this explains why it goes unspoken following a shooting.

EXPLAINING FETISHES

Few behaviors are as puzzling to the non-clinician as a *fetish*, which is an overwhelming interest by a man in a seemingly ordinary object like shoes, feet, an odor, or another article of clothing. It rarely afflicts women.

Though apparently "crazy" there is a logic to this interest since it derives from earliest childhood when the mind is most immature and the child is easily frightened. The creation of a fetish is motivated by so terrifying a sight that a *screen memory* was created to hide it in a symbol, which is the fetish. This protects them from remembering the overly exciting event, perhaps the sight of a naked female lacking a penis and which the child begins to fear they may lose and the fetish symbolizes, or of adults having sex.

While almost all adults have some irrational fear or odd interest, only those interfering with normal functioning require treatment.

THE EXHIBITIONIST SURGEON AND THE POPULAR CONCEPT OF NORMALITY

A talented psychoanalyst once described his treatment of a surgeon who persistently exhibited his genitals in public. During his therapy the patient realized that this powerfully motivated behavior reflected his early childhood desire to show his mother how powerful he was. An act which is not unusual for very young children and properly discouraged by their parents.

This patient's risky criminal behavior evidenced a generally ignored truth: that the unconscious is powerful and cannot be ignored. Still, most prefer to think that consciousness governs behavior until forced to believe otherwise.

All humans are a product of their upbringing. Thus, infantile misconceptions and fears may erupt at any time, which must be understood and controlled. Being "normal" means functioning in line with developmental expectations as youth or adult. *Not* that one is ever free of apparently inexplicable thoughts and feelings which can lead to unwise behavior.

When one responds to a situation with greater emotion than warranted, the behavior is motivated by an unconscious feeling of being humiliated, perhaps during a childhood event or as an adult on the job. Consider the unfortunately common "road rage" if you will.

HOW TO SUCCESSFULLY COPE WITH PANIC ATTACK

1. Tell yourself that your frightening feelings are *not* dangerous. That anxiety can mimic the symptoms of virtually every medical disorder and what you're experiencing is just an exaggeration of the normal anxiety response to your present excess stress.

2. Don't think about what *might* happen.

2. Remind yourself that confronting your fear will reduce its intensity and ultimately cause it to vanish.

THE DANGEROUSLY IGNORED POWER OF THE UNCONSCIOUS

An unfortunate current development is the tendency to ignore the unconscious factors affecting human behavior. Thus in today's "I'm OK, You're OK" era on steroids, virtually any belief or action has become acceptable no matter how outlandish it had been considered.

The murder attempt on Supreme Court Justice Kavanaugh evidenced the power of unconscious motivation. That the accused, twenty-six-year-old Nicholas Roske, is mentally disturbed cannot be questioned since even he admitted this. "I wouldn't say I'm thinking clearly," he said in court. Yet his preparations--acquiring pistol, pepper spray, the Justice's home address, and more, indicates coherence.

Fortunately before acting, Mr. Roske phoned the local emergency services, stated his murderous plan, and requested help. Thus the logical conscious element, what psychologists call the *Executive Function*, overcame the unconscious conflict driving him to kill.

As I often state, the unconscious is powerful and one must respect its power.

MY OLD BLACK SUIT

A newspaper article questioning whether men still wore suits during the present casual era aroused a memory.

During my training at Washington University Medical School's Child Psychiatry Department I attended a seminar taught by a gifted psychoanalyst who was idolized by students. This doctor always wore a black suit and I soon bought one.

I no longer remember ever wearing it but still have it, occasionally glancing at it in the closet and dusting it as one would a holy relic. I will *never* recycle it as the article suggests.

DEFINING PSYCHOTHERAPY AND OTHER "THERAPIES"

Therapy is now a popular term with people speaking of music therapy, art therapy, horse-back-riding therapy, and even shopping therapy. Yet though relaxing, these activities are not psychotherapy as it has long been conceived.

Ideally, a psychotherapist has been trained in child and adult psychological development and its aberrations, training these other "therapists" lack.

So when seeking permanent emotional change, you know which practitioner to call.

THE UNSPOKEN "ELEPHANT IN THE ROOM" MOTIVATING KILLINGS BY YOUTH

Recently, after yet another shooting by a teenager, New York City's Mayor Adams asked where their parents were while the youth wandered the streets at night. Or, to put it more bluntly, why were they so lacking in parental responsibility. For expressing this truth the mayor was widely criticized, which is why his sound position is greatly ignored by politicians.

That early developmental experiences are the bedrock of adult behavior is unquestioned. It is when the basic ego capacities governing thinking and behavior are formed, and for which a *good-enough* though not perfect parenting is needed with only greatly deficient parenting causing problems. Yet even here the presence of a committed inspiring relative or teacher can make a difference with a child's mind latching onto and incorporating the healthier notion of life from them.

Nor, except in extreme circumstances, should parents be blamed for their child's misbehavior since children are not born with instructions and parents are a product of their own childhood issues. After gaining treatment for their troubled child they should *not* feel guilty since they have done all that can reasonably be expected.

Thus continues the Elephant in the Room of parental responsibility from officials fearing to lose votes if uttering it.

WHY PSYCHIATRIC DIAGNOSES ARE OFTEN WORTHLESS

Frequently after news of a murder spree surfaces, report of the criminal's prior psychiatric diagnosis follows: that he had been diagnosed as psychotic or suffering from OCD (Obsessive-Compulsive Disorder) or ADHD (Attention Deficit Hyperactivity Disorder) or another. Yet the treatment which followed each diagnosis was unsuccessful and the critical question *why* remains.

Despite the complexity of human behavior this answer is simple: because naming a condition according to current diagnostic nomenclature, which is required for insurance payment, has taken the place of understanding the person, for which study of their childhood is essential but often absent.

To explain a person's behavior one must know the state of their ego capacities, which develop before the age of four-years and govern the ability to control thinking and behavior, to modulate mood, to distinguish reality from fantasy, and others, all comprising what is termed the *Executive Function*.

Yet for decades the false reductionist pseudo-neurological/chemical notion of what governs human behavior has been followed: that aberrant behavior reflects the existence of a "chemical imbalance" which is best treated with medication. Only recently has criticism of this spurious notion increased, even as crime and suffering multiply.

ASSESSING DANGEROUSNESS

After every multiple murder there is the usual criticism of why it wasn't prevented. Especially when the danger seemed clear as with a murder spree in Buffalo. But, as has long been said, everyone has twenty-twenty vision in hindsight.

Predicting suicide or homicide is difficult since despite popular belief of its frequency it is rare. While virtually all consider homicide or suicide at some point in their life, exceedingly few do with the risk factors being the seriousness of intent, the degree of control over behavior, the realism of the plan, and the availability of lethal means as a gun or poison.

During my long career in a range of clinical settings I have advised hospitalization for a literal handful of patients. I have also known many who were hospitalized inappropriately which can have a devastating psychological effect.

Risk is determined by questioning the patient and their family member(s) with the doctor's conclusion deriving from their knowledge of human development and behavior. But the accuracy of this conclusion depends on the doctor's talent and knowledge which vary greatly.

I once spoke with a worried psychiatrist at a general hospital. His patient spoke seriously of killing the American President and the doctor didn't know what to do. The hospital was equipped for only short-term psychiatric stays so the patient must soon be discharged. I advised the doctor to inform the Secret Service. He did and they whisked the patient to another hospital that day.

But mental health decisions are not always so clear-cut, nor are the appropriate facilities always available.

THE BENEFIT AND DANGER OF TUNNEL VISION

While focused concentration is prized, too great focus can be dangerous. For example, when obsessed by a personal concern, one may incautiously cross a busy street. or suicide when depressed by a job loss or romantic breakup. In these events, perspective was lost for tunnel vision predominated.

Yet tunnel vision, holding an exaggerated narrow focus, can save lives too as when traversing a crime-laden neighborhood or on the battlefield. Unhelpful tunnel vision occurs when the presenting situation is *misperceived* as a permanent rather than temporary setback or being perilous and not innocuous.

THE PREVAILING CULTURAL IGNORANCE

I've read *The Godfather* several times and listened to its audio version twice. Now more convinced than ever that it is a masterpiece of vivid characters and unbeatable plot.

That many teenagers have never heard of this classic is an example of the prevailing cultural ignorance. I have known teenagers who never heard of the Vietnam War or Winston Churchill and when referring to the renowned play, "My Fair Lady," in one of my novels, I felt compelled to describe in a footnote what it is .

Yet memory is fleeting so, no longer remembering what I knew as a teenager, perhaps my judgment on modern youth is too harsh.

THE ADVANTAGES OF AUDIO-VIDEO PSYCHOTHERAPY

While providing audio-video health services has existed for decades in the military and less populated regions, it became widespread during COVID when its benefits were revealed:

1. It is independent of weather with appointments not being missed because of poor driving conditions.

2. There is greater ease of movement with parents not needing to bring a young hanger-on, one with their own activity in mind, when seeking services.

3. There is increased ease of scheduling with the clinician no longer needing to book appointments enabling them to leave their office as early as possible.

4. When practice is conducted via audio-video from a home office, clinicians are often willing to schedule an appointment at a time they would otherwise resist if it required travel to their office. A patient once phoned for an appointment as I was leaving home. "Give me five minutes," I told her.

5. The possibility of varied treatment location: a psychotherapy session can be scheduled during a patient's lunch hour or while seated in their parked car, and a couple's session can be conducted with each is at a different location miles apart.

THE BENEFIT AND DANGER OF HOLDING AN
INACCURATE SELF IMAGE

While it is often believed that holding an incorrect concept of who one is, what psychologists term their *sense of self*, is harmful, this is not always true. Being common with emotional disorders, these sufferers do benefit since the fantasy grants them hope and protects them from despair.

Moreover, the thought may indicate an embryonic talent which could lead to significant achievement after their healing through treatment.

But while comforting, holding an unrealistic fantasy with no hope of success can lead to even greater despair.

THE ALLEGED ADHD EPIDEMIC

Attention-Deficit Hyperactivity Disorder (ADHD) is an unsophisticated notion with a long history, being termed "mental restlessness" in 1700s England and Minimal Brain Dysfunction (MBD) in early 1900s America, of which a Harvard psychiatrist then said that any doctor using this diagnosis had a minimal brain dysfunction. ADHD is its newest incarnation.

Though a large profitable industry has developed from it, ADHD symptoms are *identical* to anxiety and depression which are associated with every psychological and physical disturbance. Its growth reflects ignorance of child psychological development and the attempt to "neurologize" psychological symptoms and life issues. And check online for the often-prescribed drug potential side effects which are far from small.

Some children with school learning issues and adults with concentration difficulty *do* have psychological problems. But these reflect what has long been understood as a weakness of basic ego capacities which develop in early childhood and include control of thinking and behavior, mood modulation, and others. Psychotherapy can heal these problems by replacing the deficient ego capacities with more mature ones. These weaknesses are not a black/white, present/absent diagnosis but a continuum of strengths and weaknesses that need be assessed through interview and, when minimal, may be possessed by the most successful people.

ON THE DESERVED AND UNDESERVED GUILT FEELINGS OF PARENTS

While it is best for a distressed child to receive mental health treatment early this is not always done. Babies are not born with instructions and parental guilt is often a factor, they fearing to be judged as having played a role in the development of their child's problems.

While parents don't blame themselves for a child's physical illness they often do so with their child's emotional problems. Feeling responsible since early life experience is the bedrock of adequate later functioning.

But parenting mistakes derive from a lack of knowledge and the parent's own imperfect life experiences. So, after gaining treatment for their child, any parental feelings of guilt are undeserved and counter-productive in helping their child.

And though children readily forgive parental mistakes, they never forget or forgive that their distress had been ignored.

POST-TRAUMATIC STRESS DISORDER (PTSD) IS NOT YOUR ENEMY

Post-traumatic Stress Disorder (PTSD) has gained much of its false popular knowledge from frightening movies depicting berserk ex-soldiers on killing sprees. Yet its symptoms can develop in anyone including children.

It exists because the mind has a limited capacity to cope with stress and, when exceeded, *symptoms* develop. A symptom is the sign that something is wrong which, with PTSD, can include nightmares, flashbacks of the causative event, psychogenic seizures, over-sensitivity to startling noises, or odd fears and a repetitive thought (an *obsession*). These reflect the urgent message from the unconscious that help is needed to avoid damaging the mind or body, as continuing intense anxiety can do.

Thus, PTSD symptoms are like the bodily fever that warns of infection, being temporarily uncomfortable but critical since it motivates the sufferer to seek the treatment they need to regain their health.

*POPULAR "COMMON SENSE" ISN'T ALWAYS GOOD
PARENTING SENSE*

Some popular child guidance guidelines, long followed by parents and teachers, derive from the concept of behavior modification that reward and punishment affect behavior. Thus if a child is punished for misbehaving they are less likely to do so in the future. A belief which sounds logical but is not true.

As psychologists have long known, behavior modification works with dogs but not cats, with those of severely limited intellectual ability since it simplifies their environment, but *not* with those of near normal and above intelligence. It also works with most inhabitants of tightly controlled environments such as prisons unless they are seriously emotionally disturbed. It does *not* work with others more than briefly since humans are a thinking species.

Moreover, children are reasonable and want to develop into adults. Thus if asked to do something by their parent or teacher they usually will though being less likely to do so if they are hungry or tired or ill or troubled, or unable to do what is asked for a reason which makes sense to their immature perhaps troubled mind but not to an adult.

Thus, apart from emergency situations involving danger, explaining why a child should do something will usually gain their cooperation. If not, it will be because of one or more of the above reasons, at which time they will be behaving like similarly afflicted adults.

THE SURPRISING BENEFIT OF PANIC ATTACK

Panic Attack is the experience of extreme anxiety when the normal symptoms of anxiety are misinterpreted as a deadly medical event. Feeling so unbearable that it causes many to rush to an Emergency Room, fearing that a lethal cardiac event is developing though most are suffering only anxiety.

Yet like all psychological symptoms, Panic Attack has the value of motivating a change of behavior before bodily damage occurs. Thus an overly-stressed person who had resisted changing their life-style may seek help after suffering this distress. Later realizing what had caused it: over-work; loneliness; or even the yearning for intimacy which had been ignored but became aroused during a chance encounter.

THE FALSE BUT SEDUCTIVE ATTRACTION OF SUICIDE

Because of the instinctive biological imperative to live, suicide can be difficult to understand. Particularly when it occurs with highly successful people like the former Miss USA, Cheslie Krystal, who was also a lawyer, and the widely applauded CEO of the Atlanta rail transportation system, Jeffrey Parker. Unless one understands the psychology of despair.

Obsessed with tunnel vision by their suffering, the suicidal person sees no way to end it except through suicide, and sometimes in a manner appearing fitting for them but illogical to others. Krystal leapt from a skyscraper and Parker jumped in front of a moving train.

While the symbolization of the self-destructive means is not relevant, the earlier turning inward of the sufferer's personal world is highly significant. There are gradations of this thinking since virtually all people consider suicide at some point in their life, perhaps after receiving a serious medical diagnosis or during a particularly stressful work situation. Yet relatively few do suicide with the proverbial "needle in the haystack" being an accurate metaphor for the act.

And as has been long said, suicide is a permanent solution to a temporary problem, even that which feels unbearable at the moment.

COPING WITH LIFE REGRETS

When considering their life, every thoughtful person must regret things they did and said and feelings left unsaid. Being human, making mistakes are inevitable.

Yet accepting this truism isn't easy whether it involves losing a past, potentially great love (for there can be no certainly how a relationship would have progressed), child-rearing errors, or resentments which kept one from the critical understanding that came but only after a hated relative died.

Unfortunately, even for those who experienced the healthiest upbringing, life can be hard and the forgiveness of oneself and others can be wanting.

THE FEAR OF INTIMACY

A common complaint, about which topic there have been many self-help books, is of problems with intimacy, without which life can lack meaning.

The capacity for intimate relationships develops in early infancy, its prototype being the mother-infant interaction. If, as usually occurs, the child's wants are satisfied when needed, the child develops a positive view of intimacy and the world in general. If not, a corollary view may be established: that intimacy is dangerous and to be avoided, and the world is unfriendly.

Because early life experiences are the bedrock of personality and adult behavior, these negative feelings won't change without psychotherapy, or after a lengthy loving relationship, which can be difficult to gain when possessing these fears.

*THE VALUE OF PSYCHOLOGICAL AUTOPSY AFTER A
PUBLICIZED SUICIDE*

The motivation for suicide can be many, distress at the loss of a loved one, job stress, or another, it being most puzzling when the deceased is relatively young and successful.

I was reminded of this upon reading of the suicide of fifty-five-year-old Jeffrey Parker who successfully led the Metropolitan Atlanta Rapid Transit Authority (MARTA) after notable public service in other states. While the virtue of privacy is often ignored, conducting a psychological autopsy after a widely publicized suicide would serve the same public good as medical treatment case histories, by educating people about behavior and the power of the unconscious.

And if dissuading others from suicide they would create a fitting memorial to the deceased.

SPECIAL EDUCATION CONSIGNS STUDENTS TO A TREADMILL OF FAILURE

Long ago, while conducting research in a school, I sensed its similarity to a factory.

Both operate on a rigid timetable where products (widgets or students) must move smoothly along the production line. With students this involves moving uninterruptedly from classroom to lunchroom to dismissal with interference being removed.

Thus defective widgets, or slowly advancing or uncooperative students, are removed and sent to *Special Education*. Where, alas, they begin their struggle along the *treadmill of failure*.

The reason for this is simple: while academic failure can result from several reasons, it usually reflects psychological problems which schools are ill-equipped to remedy.

NAMING A CHILD

In my grade school class were two children with my first name. Being the only one with a middle name, I was long addressed by it. Which I hated as a teenager when a laughable teenage TV character was given this name. There was also a famed actor and a high-ranking government official with this name but I didn't know it and children don't always think logically.

Years later, while walking along the beach, I met a grade school friend cavorting with a bikini model that he knew from his job in the garment center. He immediately jumped up and ran toward me, shouting my hated middle name. To which I impulsively responded, "Shut up!"

Don't ask me this name since I still hate it though telling it to several children who vow to keep it secret.

WHY BEGINNING PSYCHOTHERAPY IS FEARED BY MANY

To begin psychotherapy is harder than to begin consulting a physician or dentist. With these professionals, people have had a lifetime of experience, knowing their routines and what will happen from the time they enter the office. But a psychotherapy office lacks its medical gadgets and aura, having homelike furnishings. Nor do most therapists in solo practice have a receptionist as in medical offices.

The procedure is also different. After the initial greeting, questions are asked with the lengthy medical office paper questionnaire being absent and length of treatment session being longer and consistent.

Yet despite the visible differences the goals of psychotherapists and medical doctors are the same: to effect healing.

THE MURDERERS AMONG US

The book, *The Killer Across The Table*, by John Douglas and Mark Olshaker, narrates their interviews of noted serial killers during which similarities were found. All had a troubled childhood, having experienced far from "good-enough" parenting with cruelty and/or sexual abuse, and often a particularly damaging relationship with their mother. Which is not surprising since the mother-child interaction is paramount during the early years when the ego capacities governing impulse control and thinking develop.

These killers had a remarkable ability for psychological "splitting," separating and walling-off one aspect of their thinking and emotional life from another. Thus they could murder a child just before volunteering to join a search party for them. This, even while feeling concern that their child get to school.

Rage and power were the dominant motives even in killings with a sexual element. The killer of a young girl who came to their home to deliver Girl Scout cookies, knew from the moment he opened the door that he would kill her. This man, a high school teacher who lived with his mother, had been told she would refuse to see him and cut him from her will if he ever married. This threat caused him to break his engagement and added to his two types of rage. One that he could control when a driver cut him off. But the second that he could not, when the unlucky girl came to his home.

Another killer repeated his crime after being paroled following his rape and murder of a young woman. That these killers are not insane (which is a legal term) is evidenced by the care they took to avoid being caught during the murder and disposal of the body.

The book stressed several things: 1. The crucial need for more accurate assessment of those who are arrested; 2. To consider even such unlikely suspects as family friends and relatives as the potential culprit; 3. To take reported suspicions seriously since many killing sprees would have been ended earlier had this been done, particularly of killings by medical staff in hospitals.

The authors state that all serial killers: have psychological conflict causing their feelings about themselves to vary between grandiosity and inadequacy; possess a sense of personal entitlement which causes them to feel they need not follow society's laws; and can choose, which makes them deserving of capital punishment.

RITTENHOUSE AND THE COMMON TEENAGE FANTASY

On August 25, 2020, Kyle Rittenhouse, a 17-year-old from Antioch, Illinois, fatally shot two men and wounded another in Kenosha, Wisconsin. The shootings occurred during the protests, riots, and civil unrest following the shooting of Jacob Blake. Rittenhouse, armed with an AR-15 style rifle, had joined a group of armed people in Kenosha who said they were there to protect businesses.

Despite public clamor about Rittenhouse's actions, there has been no exploration of how these relate to the common adolescent yearning to improve the world, which is sometimes indicated in their dreams by an explosion. This doesn't mean the dreamer wants to blow up something but rather their desire to change the world. Which seems for them possible because of their limited experience, though adults can hold it too. Once, during a workshop at the National Institute of Mental Health in Washington, I was so floored by the expertise of the government speakers that I naively believed our group could accomplish *anything*.

Perhaps seventeen-year-old Rittenhouse, when taking up his rifle and medic kit to protect a community, was driven by a similar fantasy, which is understandable since he had worked as a lifeguard.

But as many adults and few teenagers tend to realize, events don't always proceed according to plan.

EMOTIONAL DESENSITIZATION AFTER TRAUMA

A common characteristic of Post-Traumatic Stress Disorder (PTSD) is emotional desensitization, being unable to experience the feelings that make us human such as warmth, closeness, and joy in relationships. What feeling is experienced is rage which may be expressed through self-defeating or even violent behavior, the mind having created this emotional blockage as a survival/self-protective mechanism after the frightening, paralyzing trauma.

The extreme behavior that can follow reflects the anger of frustration and attempts to smash this blockage of feelings, to feel *something*. This emotional blockage can derive from military combat or the civilian experience of an adult or a child, from terrorist bombing or the child abuse by grossly inadequate parenting.

Providing understanding of the nature of emotional desensitization will increase the likelihood of its healing.

HOW PARENTS CAN EXPLAIN SCARY DREAMS TO THEIR CHILD

Though scary dreams frighten and can upset, "They are our friends" I tell my young patients. Being stories that our mind creates to tell us what is bothering us and, like the mystery movies that we love, we should try to figure out.

A scary dream might mean that we are upset about school the next day or about learning a new task like swimming. Or even of growing up and leaving home, which is a common worry as one grows older.

Explaining nightmares in this manner reassures a child, reduces their fear, and creates their belief that if scary dreams don't frighten their parents they are not to be feared at all.

Once, having spoken this way to a five-year-old girl and repeating myself a month later after her scary dream, she dismissively said, "Oh I know *that*!"

THE HAVANA SYNDROME, ANXIETY, AND THE POWER OF THE UNCONSCIOUS

There has been much publicity about what has been termed the *Havana Syndrome*: debilitating physical and cognitive symptoms allegedly caused by electronic waves projected by foreign agents. So certain is this explanation that doctors who differ by relating these symptoms to psychological causes are ridiculed. This, despite experts insisting that no evidence of such a weapon has been found or that they are even conceptually possible.

I have no special knowledge of the Havana Syndrome nor do I wish to minimize the pain of its sufferers. Yet the power of the unconscious generally tends to be minimized with all preferring to believe they have ultimate power over their behavior. Which is true except when stress or emotions overpower it and when physical symptoms may occur.

Many rushing to an Emergency Room fearing a cardiac event are really suffering the extreme anxiety of Panic Attack during which the normal symptoms of anxiety are *misinterpreted* as a deadly medical event.

Anxiety symptoms can mimic virtually every physical disorder, even causing visual symptoms when stress causes an optical migraine. Nature behaves economically, having adapted bodily systems to multiple uses with a large gland like the liver performing hundreds of tasks from processing glucose to generating hemoglobin. A woman suffered recurring nightmares from which she awoke screaming with marks on her wrists.

Identical to those which developed when, as a child, she was repeatedly held down by her wrists and sexually abused.

The unconscious is powerful, and one must respect its power.

RECURRING NIGHTMARES AND THEIR ELIMINATION

Dreaming occurs nightly but dreams are not always remembered. The more disturbing the dream, the more likely is to be remembered and dreams can be painful indeed.

One five-year-old dreamed repeatedly of being eaten by wild animals, and an adult's recurring dream mirrored her sexual abuse as a child. Yet eliminating painful dreams is not rocket science since dreaming has long been understood. And despite their occasional discomfort, all dreams are "our friends," as I tell my young patients. They are movies created by our mind to tell what is troubling us, perhaps fear of an upcoming school test or learning to swim or the like.

Interpreting a recurring nightmare, whether of a child or an adult, will usually eliminate it. *Unless* the interpretation was faulty or incomplete, there being more to the emotional conflict that it symbolizes, or the person cannot tolerate confronting the conflict at that time in their life.

One adult's nightmare lasted for decades, taking years-apart interpretations before finally disappearing, important personality changes having to occur first. The initial interpretation reduced the nightmare's frequency but a timely, second interpretation was required to eliminate it completely.

There is a logic to nightmares just as with physical symptoms. A fever disappears when the infection causing it is gone and a nightmare vanishes when the emotional conflict that it symbolizes is resolved.

WHY FANCIFUL EXPLANATIONS OF AUTISM PERSIST

While parents rarely feel guilty when their child becomes physically ill, this is not true when they develop emotional problems. This guilt is perhaps most prevalent with autism which, in its severest form, can devastate family life.

Recent infant research has confirmed what clinicians long suspected: that early parent-child interaction plays an overwhelming role in its development. Yet, denial of this fact persists and we read of continuing, failed attempts to relate autism to vaccination or pollution or whatever, to *any* cause but parenting. Which is understandable since the sight of a severely autistic child horrifies and no parent would willingly accept blame for this.

All children possess psychological strengths and limitations, as do parents who had their own childhood struggles. The parents' personalities must mesh with their unselected newborn so mismatches naturally occur. But once a child's emotional problem is recognized and help for it is sought, *any* parental feeling of guilt is undeserved and counter-productive to the success of treatment.

A positive thought is that autism is vastly over-diagnosed. In my long experience in medical and psychological settings, I have seen fewer than five severely disturbed, self-mutilating autistic children and fewer than twenty accurately diagnosed autistic children with lesser symptoms. Moreover, young children whose behavior exhibit some autistic features can have these symptoms disappear through ordinary play psychotherapy, and sometimes in just a few months. With lengthy skillful services, major change can be made in even the most disturbed autistic child's life.

FAILURE AND SUCCESS IN THE TREATMENT OF AUTISTIC CHILDREN

The aloofness noted in autistic children can become a self-fulfilling prophecy if their therapist considers it a given, and especially if their behavior is considered amenable only to simplistic reward-punishment/behavior modification technique. But the autistic child *does* have relationships though these are inadequate and require nurturing through play psychotherapy.

No special treatment technique is needed since the basic difficulty of autistic children is communication and play is the primary language in conducting psychotherapy with young children.

Thus autistic children must be related to individually, with their aloofness not being taken as a rejection of interpersonal contact but merely their inadequacy at it. A recent study found that most infants who had communication difficulties associated with autism during their second year were later no longer diagnosable as autistic when their mothers were given early intense instruction in how to communicate with them.

*WHY THE UNSOPHISTICATED ADHD DIAGNOSIS
PERSISTS*

The Attention-Deficit Hyperactivity Disorder (ADHD) diagnosis persists despite it possibly being the most unsophisticated notion in mental health for the past two-hundred-years. In the late 1700s an English physician described the symptoms as "mental restlessness." In early 20th century America they were described as reflecting Minimal Brain Dysfunction (MBD), this causing a Harvard psychiatrist to remark that any doctor using this diagnosis had a minimal brain dysfunction.

ADHD is its latest incarnation and makes no sense with more such diagnoses existing on the East Coast than the West Coast and of boys than girls. This, apart from its symptoms being *identical* to anxiety and depression which are present in every serious medical and psychological condition.

When these symptoms are present, whether in children or adults and unrelated to such worry, they reflect what is professionally termed *Elements of a Borderline Psychotic Psychostructural Organization*. Which does not mean Psychotic or Borderline Psychotic but the weakness of basic ego capacities because of faulty developmental experiences during the first three years of life and affect control of behavior and thinking.

The ADHD diagnosis has persisted, I believe, for several reasons: 1. Large, profitable mental health and pharmaceutical industries have grown up around it. 2. Ego psychology has grown out of favor with a dearth of education of clinicians about early child psychological development. My doctoral advisor once said that to understand human behavior one must go to psychoanalytic concepts, that there is nowhere else to go and I agree. 3. Sixty years ago most psychiatrists provided psychotherapy. Today few do apart from those who have undergone psychoanalytic training. So today's psychiatrists mostly prescribe drugs which, sadly, some parents demand and doctors comply. As a mother once told me, she would rather her child had a brain tumor than emotional problems since a tumor could be cut out. Many new patients don't understand what emotional problems or psychotherapy are and must be educated.

A GIRL-FRIEND'S MURDER AND FREUD'S BENEDICTION

While not downplaying the power of unconscious motivation, the murder of many abused women might have been avoided had they followed one simple rule: to better know their partner before becoming intimate.

Nearly a hundred-years ago, an unmarried American psychiatrist underwent his training analysis with Freud in Vienna. At their last meeting, Freud expressed the wish that the doctor be lucky enough to gain a happy marriage. "With all your psychological knowledge is luck a factor?" the surprised doctor asked. "Of course, because one does not really know another person without living with them for a long time," Freud replied.

Thus my advice to all: it takes a long time to know someone. *Take it* before committing yourself to a relationship.

THE INEXHAUSTABLE STRENGTH OF MOTHERS

My experience treating mothers has long impressed me with their strengths. Despite their continuing daily tasks of tending to wandering-about youngsters, coping with sometimes seemingly incomprehensible teenagers, difficult husbands and an occasional sickly rabbit or other pet, they cook, clean, negotiate with school officials, provide transportation to appointments, and cope with such intermittent crises as helping with children's homework and arranging for home repairs. All while trying and often failing to care for themselves during their "free time," when not working at paid employment of course.

Part of this is inevitable since, in most families, the mother is the emotional center of the family, making her the major recipient of children's complaints. If a child is unhappy, it's *her* fault. Is this fair? Of course not but that's how it is.

Which is not to say that the father's role is unimportant. Though the mother (or mothering figure who can be a male) is the most important figure during the first two years of a child's life, the father becomes equally important during their third year, serving to pull the child from its symbiotic relationship with their mother into the larger world and, ultimately, independent adult functioning.

WHY SOME YOUTH CAN BENEFIT FROM PSYCHOTHERAPY AND OTHERS CAN'T

Critical psychological development occurs during early life and may not later happen even if the patient is treated by the most talented psychotherapist.

Change is difficult and some youth cannot tolerate the inherent dependency of treatment. A teenager may need a firmer path in life before accepting this childhood-like experience they struggle to escape though there is a great difference between the two.

Unlike with parents, a therapist does not make demands. Their sole goal is that their patient's goals be achieved so long as they are healthy and of which they may be unaware.

For some youth, completing their education through college or graduate school or technical training comes first. Until then they try to ignore their distress, *depressing it* until the better day when they feel confident of independent and financial survival in the adult world.

WHAT THE DEADLY DISORDER OF ANOREXIA REALLY REFLECTS

A major function of early childhood is for the child to develop a secure sense of who they are, a process which normally occurs naturally through their continuous interaction with their parents.

If these were inadequate, the child's immaturely developed ego capacities are unable to cope with stress and particularly with the later powerful feelings that impinge adolescents. Thus, a de-compensation, "falling apart," may occur comprising symptoms that can range from low self-esteem to identity confusion to, rarely, personality disintegration (psychosis).

Anorexic symptoms typically begin in adolescence when there is a need to integrate powerful feelings within the personality. Feeling vulnerable and a loss of control over their body, something which the ego's *Executive Function* provides, the teenager tries to bolster their self-esteem and gain a sense of control over their body through concrete behaviors: obsessively focusing on their body through their diet, and constantly exercising.

Because the anorexic person isn't aware of the connection between their symptoms and fragmented self, they tend to resistant psychotherapy. This, despite anorexia having the highest death rate of all mental health conditions.

Then, symptoms occur with low self-esteem being the least severe. More troubling are confusion about their identity or even personality disintegration (psychosis).

A recent harrowing news story described an anorectic woman who felt so worn down by her social isolation and painful treatments that she sought assisted suicide though being only in her thirties.

NORMAL LINGERING GRIEF

Watching the Netflix documentary on the 2001 terror attack on the World Trade Centers aroused my teary memories: from seeing posted photos of missing loved ones who were almost certainly dead, and at a later memorial at Judson Church. I experienced this though knowing none who died in the attack. My sister-in-law escaped through chance, being absent from her job at the World Trade Center because of jury duty that fateful morning.

Contrary to popular belief, there is no normal way to grieve. Immediately after a death some cry, others only cry years later, and some never do. Having dreams in which the deceased lives and speaks is common.

The anniversary of a loved one's death can have a powerful impact with some tearfully describing it long after. A close relative's death occasionally has a positive effect, liberating healthy autonomy strivings from an overpowering, destructively possessive relationship.

REDUCING THE TERROR OF PSYCHOLOGICAL SYMPTOMS AND LENGTH OF TREATMENT

The treatment of a psychological disorder is often long. Yet, to paraphrase Freud's comment of more than a hundred years ago, it would be nice to have a rapid cure for deadly medical disorders too.

But the problems of living do differ. A traumatic event troubling a previously healthy person may require only one to two months of psychotherapy but far longer if caused by a lifetime of distress.

It is important during treatment to relate current (adult) symptoms to the unhealthy developmental experiences that produced them. This enables the patient to understand their life and why they repeat their mistakes. It also reduces their fear that anxiety or depression might invade their consciousness at any time.

All symptoms exist for a logical reason, vanishing as does fever when the illness causing it ends. Thus, understanding the unconscious conflict that arouses symptoms reduces their terror and gives hope.

WHY YOUR CHILD IS SOMETIMES "IMPOSSIBLE"

While all children irritate sometime, they are occasionally impossible. I've joked with parents that the hair salon business next to mine had a Saturday swap meet for parents to exchange children.

But a child's troublesome behavior does have meaning since they don't normally speak of their distress when unhappy but instead behave nastily. This is why *Oppositional-Defiant Behavior* is a frequent mental health diagnosis of children.

When asked to do something by their parent or teacher a child will usually comply since they *want* to grow up, to become an adult. Resistance indicates their inability to do what is asked because of illness, exhaustion, emotional upset, hunger, or for a unique psychological reason making sense to them but not to an adult.

Then, speaking quietly with the child is more productive than yelling, which should only be done during a potentially dangerous situation. *Frequent* parental yelling will cause critical warnings to be ignored.

THE UNAVOIDABLE STRESS OF BEING A NEW PARENT

While a child's birth is joyously anticipated, their parents' initial reaction is stress. This, even with a child who is easy to parent since their parents' pain is both universal and unavoidable.

Even from the womb a newborn makes continuing demands that their mother be a more effective caretaker. Communicating this by causing her bodily discomfort.

After birth, the demands for attention and more are critical since the baby is wholly dependent on their parents for survival. But the adult mind is conservative and innately resists the rapid personality change that is demanded. This clashing of wills creates parental stress, which slowly lessens as the needs of the child and their parents meld.

An added stress is that the newborn is inserted into a family social system that developed over time and must now transform itself to incorporate an unselected newcomer.

*PENTAGON POLICE OFFICER KILLED - DANGEROUS WITH
ANY BAIL*

News of a Pentagon police officer's murder was even more
shocking after learning the prior behavior of his killer. Twenty-
seven-year-old Austin W, Lanz had been arrested for trespassing
and burglary after breaking into a neighbor's home where
security cameras recorded him leaving inappropriate pictures
and messages in their mailbox. He took nothing but spoke of
police aircraft flying over the neighborhood and his phone being
tracked.

While being booked into jail, and without provocation, he
attacked and seriously injured two sheriff's deputies, then asked
that his restraints be removed so he could fight them one-by-one.
After being charged with aggravated battery on police, making a
terrorist threat, and rioting in a penal institution, he was released
on $30,000 bail, ordered to submit to a mental health
evaluation, and barred from using alcohol or drugs and
possessing firearms. For all the good this did!

While hindsight has 20/20 vision as the adage insists, one can't
help wondering why Mr. Lanz wasn't hospitalized or jailed. The
failure of legal restraint against impulsive, disturbed criminals is
countless as evidenced by the frequent murder of divorced
women by their former partner, road rage, and assaults on
strangers though these can't be wholly stopped. A colleague once
told me of a psychiatrist who had been eating in the cafeteria
when he was attacked by a patient with whom he had no prior
contact.

The only possible explanation for these disastrous judicial decisions is that many still won't believe that some people are, perhaps only temporarily, inherently dangerous. Thus, the failure to respect the power of the unconscious despite its frequent deadly reminders continues.

THE INESCAPABLE PAIN AND BENEFITS OF ANXIETY AND DEPRESSION

While the pain of anxiety and depression cannot be denied, neither can it be avoided since both are part of the human condition, enabling us to become more fully human and more of who we can be.

Anxiety signals impending danger, both actual and real, trying to protect one from harm. An unrealistic danger indicates that an unconscious conflict, which can be anything, is causing distress. Perhaps the desire for intimacy conflicting with its fear because of early life experiences which are the bedrock of the adult personality.

Depression indicates a *depressing* of feelings for one of three reasons: being "stuck" because of an inability to decide what to do; sensing that one has deep problems and giving up; or having unsuccessfully attempted to emotionally reach a parent during childhood which can create persisting feelings of inadequacy affecting later functioning.

Making significant life changes requires confronting the unconscious conflicts which can afflict anyone, for possessing these are also part of being human.

THE AMAZING POWER OF THE UNCONSCIOUS MIND

Long ago a co-worker revealed a persisting nightmare which caused her to wake up several times a week, screaming in panic. These dreams replicated her childhood experience of being held by her wrists and sexually abused.

The mind has the power to move blood to parts of the body and, upon awakening, there were marks on her wrists where in the dream the attacker held her down.

As I often state, the unconscious is powerful and one must respect its power.

THE PSYCHOANALYTIC ROOTS OF MODERN PSYCHOTHERAPY

Classical psychoanalytic treatment, having multiple treatment sessions a week while lying on a couch, has declined since the 1970s though belief in its basic concepts of the power of the unconscious and the persistence of childhood trauma continue.

These explain our tendency to form rapid judgments. Quickly deciding if a friend is "good" or "bad" and, if the latter, instantly removing them from online "friend" status. Behavior analogous to infants who relate to their mother in black/white terms depending on whether she satisfies their momentary need. Only with maturing does a child understand that one can possess good *and* bad characteristics, and some adults possessing emotional difficulties never do.

The common adult wish that they had greater self-knowledge as a youth reflects both the benefit of life experience and the protective function of the unconscious. Because the emotional effect of an unhealthy childhood can be great, the unconscious creates false explanations to protect self-esteem and avoid the despair that might even cause suicide. Only after positive development has occurred can many allow themselves to realize their earlier emotional deficits.

But not only of former psychotherapy patients is this true. Many at the end of their life are amazed by how they endured the difficult, painful course over which they traveled.

CRIME, MURDER, AND MAYHEM

During my first job at a psychiatric hospital, I told my psychoanalyst/supervisor what my adolescent patient said. "That's psychotic," the doctor replied. Though able to define *psychotic,* until that moment I hadn't grasped the power of this condition.

Similarly, when a horrible crime becomes public, the perpetrator is usually viewed with surprise since they look so normal, lacking the twisted features of horror film characters and speaking coherently though of bogus beliefs. Columnists then ask their usual question, "Why," and provide their usual answer "No one knows," which is not true.

While predicting violence can never be certain, it correlates highly with several factors: failure in life; substance abuse; the psychological (ego) capacities governing thinking and behavior being inadequately developed; and having a fragmented *sense of self* or sense of who one is, with the killer's frequent decision to suicide being considered preferable to their continued painful existence.
'

Even an individual who committed a horrendous act is often not considered *insane* since this is a legal term determined by state statute. Most usually if they can distinguish right from wrong and, contrary to popular belief, it rarely succeeding as a legal defense.

But to describe these individuals as *sane* does not imply they possess normal control over their behavior. Still, having emotional problems except for those possessing extreme psychological limitations, should not influence their punishment. There is evil in the world and some succumb to its temptation.

WHY THE TREATMENT OF AUTISTIC CHILDREN OFTEN FAILS

Children become capable of speaking their nation's language not by learning that one word follows another but because the mind can innately induct its grammatical structure. Which is understandable since the purpose of cognition is to make sense of the personal world as quickly as possible.

Similarly, autistic children do not avoid communication but rather try to communicate in their own way. Thus, treating them with the same behavioral/ behavior-modification techniques used with an animal is doomed to failure. Instead, one must enter their personal world and wean them into the larger world, one without the painful developmental experiences that originally drove them from it.

One caution: the misdiagnosis of autism is *widespread* and play psychotherapy, the usual mode of treatment with children, can often reduce or eliminate the presence of a few autistic symptoms in mere months.

TREATING THE "DIAGNOSTICALLY HOPELESS"
PSYCHIATRIC PATIENT

To successfully treat those with severe psychological disorders, the therapist must take little for granted, ignore accepted beliefs about prognosis and motivation since clinician prejudice can arouse unjustified feelings of defeatism and hopelessness.

Each person is unique with others being unable to fully know their experience and depth of suffering. The more damaged patient knows much about themselves but, from guilt or fear of acting-out impulsively, is afraid to permit themselves to feel what they know. Nor do they value this knowledge because of their low self-esteem. Thus do they retreat from what is most useful: *to feel what they know.*

So when a patient refers to the alleged hopelessness of their prior diagnoses, they should be reminded that they are a complex human being and not a simplistic diagnostic classification.

WHEN A CHILD COMPLAINS TO THEIR PARENT

Parent-child communication isn't always straightforward. The only thing that a parent can be sure of is if their child complains of feeling ill and it is evidenced by fever or another symptom. Otherwise, a child's complaint may be valid or indirect, which is like the behavior of adults.

Consider the man who was asked to buy something by his wife and "forgot." This may be accurate if he has pressing issues on his mind or be an indirect expression of anger by behaving passive-aggressively. Similarly, a youth's puzzling behavior or statement can express a concern about the parent or another which they fear to openly express. Perhaps wanting greater independence than the parent allows or to react against what they interpret as the parent's deprecating comment.

As I never tire of repeating, the unconscious is very powerful and one must respect its power.

HOW TO SURVIVE TESTIFYING IN COURT

Testifying in court is stressful and even just being there can be nerve-racking. During my first visit to a judge's chambers I asked where to sit though this was obvious. Yet, with experience, I came to enjoy testifying in court as the government's expert witness since my information helped all participants. The more accurate information that a judge receives the better will be their decision.

Making a mistake while testifying can elicit judicial wrath and more. The following tips will help avoid this.

1. *Never* lie when testifying since the consequence can be severe. A New York psychologist who needlessly embellished his credentials, lost his license after the opposing attorney's investigation and complaint.

2. *Never* express anger when testifying since this works against you. Remain calm no matter how upsetting or even ridiculous is the attorney's question. Which is not personal since he's only doing his job.

3. *Prepare yourself* before testifying since winging it in court can be problematic even for a lawyer. After describing the nature of the Thematic Apperception Test, a psychological instrument in which a subject must tell what is happening in a drawing, the lawyer asked me, "Well, Dr. Goldstein, if I said (I no longer remember what he said), would this mean that I had sexual difficulty with my wife?" I could hardly believe what he said. He opened his mouth and the unconscious flowed out, With a

straight face I responded, "Sir, I can express no professional opinion about your sexual adequacy with your wife." The courtroom erupted in laughter and even the judge smiled though I probably should have avoided temptation since there is no laughter indicator in court transcription.

Remember that every new experience creates some degree of anxiety. Thus, because most people experience a courtroom only once if ever in their life, discomfort should be expected upon entering it.

CHOOSING A THERAPIST FOR YOUR "IMPOSSIBLE" CHILD

Children will usually be cooperative unless they're hungry, tired, ill, or emotionally unable to do what a parent requests. This is because they *want* to grow up, to behave in an adult fashion.

So when a child continually misbehaves it is because they are unhappy, because their parents are not providing what they desperately need. Yet determining what this is may not be simple and require professional advice.

My suggestion for this unaccustomed situation that you may face: if, during the first session, the clinician revels in jargon, is unable to explain in easily understandable language why your child is unhappy and its remedy, *seek another specialist! You* are the customer who must be satisfied and not the other way around.

CAN ADULT ADHD REALLY BE A PARALYZING FEAR OF FEAR?

There is no more unsophisticated, longer-lasting diagnosis than Attention Deficit Hyperactivity Disorder (ADHD) which was described two-hundred-years ago as "mental restlessness," later as Minimal Brain Dysfunction (MBD), and most recently as ADHD. This, despite its diagnostic symptoms of anxiety, depression, and concentration difficulty being present in nearly all serious medical and psychological disorders.

Unsurprisingly, adult ADHD has now become a popular diagnosis, often resulting in treatment with stimulant medication having potential side effects of seizure, stroke, abnormal heartbeat, and change of mood.

But concentration difficulty which exists since childhood may also reflect a paralyzing fear of fear, a heightened sensitivity to anxiety against which normal psychological mechanisms had never developed due to early life stress. Then, during later thoughtful work, the person experiences their sense of who they are, their *sense of self*, and becomes frightened since it indicates their long-term problem.

Relieving this in an adult, without lengthy psychotherapy to replace their deficient ego capacities with more mature ones, may be gained with the same technique used to battle many fears: understanding its nature and engaging in the feared activity in a controlled situation.

Thus, one who has difficulty concentrating should practice concentrated work for a short time each day. And, as their fear of impending anxiety lowers, their ability to concentrate may improve. Being cost-free and lacking the potentially harmful side-effects of medication, this technique is certainly worth a try.

BECOMING A NEW PARENT AND THEN CHANGING AGAIN

Becoming a parent involves both bearing a child and accepting a new identity, an expected identity and new behavior too. If, soon after birth, one asked a mother or father if they felt like a parent they would reply "no" and likely answer similarly several months later since they had not yet incorporated parenting into their self-image and range of behavior. The young parents must battle to safeguard an *area of self* against the demands of their baby-intruder.

Then, years later when their child leaves the home and deprives them of the caretaking role, the opposite happens and the parent must re-discover and re-mold their sense of who they are.

Slowly, throughout life, multiple behaviors and new functions are added to this expanding sense of self: the being as sexual, the being as worker, and the being as parent. All intertwined, like how the body metabolizes food to make it usable before incorporating its nutrition.

THE HEALTHY BENEFITS OF PAINFUL PTSD SYMPTOMS

The COVID pandemic brought Post-traumatic Stress Disorder (PTSD) to the attention of many and its potential upset was considerable: distressing thoughts and nightmares; recollections of the traumatic event(s) which may include reliving them through illusions and dissociative flashbacks; avoiding conversations about the event(s) or places they occurred; marked anxiety causing problems with sleep, concentration, and functioning on the job.

Yet though painful, these symptoms are intended by the mind to be helpful since they serve two critical functions: forcing into consciousness that the person's tolerance for stress has been exceeded and change must be made; and instigating its healthy attempt to re-integrate, to repair itself from the damage caused by intolerable stress.

The unconscious is powerful and one must respect its power.

CONFRONTING ADOLESCENT EVIL

Recent attacks on cars by bicycle riding teenagers in mid-town Manhattan caused a taxi driver thousands of dollars in damage and terrorized a family. Yet this is unsurprising during these days when society's expectation of personal responsibility has diminished. Even more surprising was the mere official call for "consequences," and a victim's hope that the perpetrators wouldn't be jailed.

The psychological capacities that enable a person to distinguish reality from fantasy, modulate mood, develop a secure identity, and control their behavior and thinking develop within the first three years of life. For this healthy growth a *good-enough* though not perfect parenting is required. Which, if lacked, reduce the likelihood of surmounting the critical adolescent goals of separating from parents, constructing realistic educational and vocational goals, and exploring intimacy through dating. These failures produce frustration and angry behavior, though rarely like that of these teenagers which, according to local shopkeepers, was not their first outrage.

As has long been known, exemplary adults can arise from impoverished families since it is the parenting that counts. The famed, recently deceased, Black economist, Walter E, Williams, credited his achievements to having had a demanding mother and teachers "who didn't give a damn about my self-esteem." His mother must have taught him values too.

No matter how great the distress, destructive behavior should not be engaged in nor tolerated by society. All parents do their best, have had their own imperfect childhood and will make mistakes though only some are inexcusable.

A school's structure and rules enable psychologically damaged youth to function better, and society relies on the police and law for this in the larger society. Yet, regardless of personal inadequacies, evil cannot be tolerated and must be condemned and punished since no desirable society can survive lacking this.

SILICON VALLEY DISCOVERS HYPNOSIS

An article in *The Wall Street Journal* talked of Silicon Valley's financing of startups marketing hypnosis apps to reduce pandemic-caused stress. Yet hypnosis is a long-accepted technique for alleviating such painful conditions as cancer, burns, headaches, and childbirth. It is even taught to asthmatic children since the less stress they experience the less likely they are to have an asthma attack.

Basically, hypnosis is *selective attention* with some researchers considering it a learned reaction and others a different physiological state. I have long believed the latter based on my personal experience, feeling a "drop" at some point during its induction and later being reluctant to "wake-up."

About ninety-percent of the population can use hypnosis to reduce stress, with ten-percent of these being such good subjects that major surgery can be performed under hypnosis. Ten-percent of the population can't be hypnotized. A quick test of hypnotic suggestibility is asking whether the subject lost themselves in reading as a child, they usually being good hypnotic subjects. Using hypnosis to lose weight or stop smoking depends on motivation and rapid change should not be expected. Those who accomplish this quickly are extraordinarily well-motivated.

Several warnings: (1) Do not be a subject for a hypnosis event in a club or on a cruise ship. While the hypnotists are often skillful, there have been cases in which not all their suggestions were eliminated with the subject winding up in an Emergency Room weeks later complaining of weird symptoms no one can figure out; (2) Do not use hypnosis while wearing contact lenses; (3) Do not listen to a hypnosis audio while driving. Though not falling asleep, you won't be fully attentive to the driving task.

With these cautions, hypnosis is safe though best learned with professional guidance. The American Society of Clinical Hypnosis can be contacted for a local practitioner.

On a personal note, decades ago a nurse taking the blood pressure of workers at my job advised that mine was high. A physician who I had known since adolescence agreed, saying that if it stayed that way I could take medication, which I adamantly opposed. Taking my blood pressure frequently would yield more accurate readings, he added, abnormally high readings being common in a doctor's office.

I followed his advice and frequently used a self-hypnotic relaxation audio which I made from the research protocol in a journal article. My blood pressure readings became optimal after two months and have remained so. By graphing these readings I found that my systolic reading (the higher number, force of blood against the artery walls) correlated with my pulse rate while my diastolic reading (the lower number, heart's resting rate or blood pressure between heartbeats) was independent of both. Digital blood pressure monitors are cheap and it is wise to monitor blood pressure at home.

AUTISM AND CREATIVITY

Dr. Baron-Cohen, author of *The Pattern Seekers: How Autism Drives Human Invention,* has found an association between autism and the capacity for hyper-systematizing, the ability to see patterns where others cannot, which is important in creative invention.

Yet it is important to keep in mind that these individuals are a *tiny* minority of all sufferers of autism, that autism is vastly mis-diagnosed and of a wide range and, when severe, is perhaps the most disabling of all mental health conditions. This, because it originates in earliest life when the mind is most immature and psychological capacities form which become bedrock of functioning.

THE UNACKNOWLEDGED BENEFITS OF DELUSIONAL THINKING

A middle-aged woman told her physician, "I've never had a chronic illness and don't think I can get one." "That's a good delusion. Keep it," the doctor replied. Yet delusions have a bad history, being popularly associated with horrific scenes from countless horror movies and murderous real-life events too. But delusional thinking can have benefits.

A person whose life has been a succession of personal disasters from psychiatric hospitalizations to painful injury to poverty develops the delusion that the FBI is watching them. Similarly, a soldier on the battlefield, close by comrades who are being killed, tells themselves they will survive. In the first example, the delusion may protect the person from suicide, since they must be important and worth respect if the FBE is watching them. And a soldier's delusion of certain longevity keeps them fighting and increases their and their comrades' probability of survival.

But delusional thinking is generally destructive since only through reality-based thinking can the problems of living be resolved. It is logical that painful anxiety and depression accompany delusional thinking since these thoughts reduce adaptability and thus increases peril.

SURVIVING PSYCHOLOGICAL DAMAGE THROUGH CREATIVITY

The stress of creativity has been long known. Dedicated artists struggle all their lives, seeking financial success which is rarely achieved, motivated by what I have termed *creative addiction.*

But creativity, though not healing, can grant meaning to an artist's life, rescuing them from life-long despair as they seek perfection in their work. These have included such survivors of dreadful childhoods as Edvard Munch and Thomas Wolfe.

Munch led a nomadic life and Wolfe's relationships were notoriously troubled as both unconsciously sought, through their creations, the idyllic childhood they yearned for and lacked as children.

THE LONG ARM OF TRAUMATIC EXPERIENCE

Thirty-years ago I was asked by an insurance company to treat an eight-year-old child who, stricken with leukemia, had been discharged from the hospital to die at home. Though fearing the emotional turmoil, I felt unable to refuse this request, feeling that he needed someone.

Holding an enamel tray lest he vomit, the boy looked terrible at our first meeting. I introduced him to the stuffed animals in my office, "our friends," as we played a board game. He looked healthy at the following two sessions, not bringing the tray and interacting with *our friends* as did my other young patients. Seeming so normal I embraced the delusion that his diagnosis was wrong and he wasn't dying. When he became too ill to travel, I went to his home and spoke with his parents in the kitchen while he slept in the bedroom.

My body reacted quickly when he died. Though healthy, I developed an unpredictable explosive diarrhea which made me unable to perform my duty as expert psychologist witness in court. Yet medical tests found nothing wrong and when the diarrhea ended two months later I sensed that it was gone forever and it never returned. Had my body tried to expel the poisonous stress through diarrhea? I wondered. A primitive reaction explained by psychosomatic medicine which long held that what is not spoken will be expressed through the body.

Twenty-six-years later an adult was referred to me for treatment. Having experienced extensive surgery, he was being heavily medicated by his doctor for pain and self-medicating himself with forbidden alcohol and cigarettes. Being a troublesome hanger-out in her office, she referred him to me "for therapy." A first glance told me he was dying. He had no interest in therapy, I didn't see him long, and my blood pressure became elevated.

A week later, without conscious intent, I spontaneously spoke of the boy who departed life too soon, leaving his parents and me to grieve. Then I did cry, and my vital signs returned to normal.

OVERCOMING AGITATED DEPRESSION

There are few more painful experiences than agitated depression, the combined anxiety and depression that can follow common trauma such as divorce, unemployment, or even apparently nothing since the unconscious is powerful.

Because feelings reflect both mind and body, they cannot be separated. Thus, remaining in bed makes depression worse and incoherent flight increases panic. But by altering the body through constructive activity like involvement in a work or household chore, agitated depression diminishes and, sometime later, its underlying reason may rise to consciousness.

THE NORMAL FEELING OF OMNIPOTENCE AND PHYSICAL ILLNESS

Physical illness involves *feeling* different, being disconnected from the usual experience of possessing control over oneself, having the ability to reason, and feeling omnipotent in the world. Though unrealistic, this sense of being all-powerful is needed since it enables functioning, the engaging in needed routines without anxiety. Yet this critical belief can be disrupted by physical change, even one so insignificant as the sufferings of an ordinary cold or stomach upset since these deny the person the feeling of intactness and affect reasoning.

Suffering a severe illness is far worse since, during this, thinking processes change and helplessness ensues with the latter being the scariest of all feelings: when the ill person becomes passive for their body no longer respects their commands.

THE PSYCHOLOGICAL PAIN OF SERIOUS ILLINESS

A TV celebrity spoke of the anxiety and depression he felt upon learning his diagnosis of pancreatic cancer. These feelings are common when serious illness threatens and after a cognitive or physical disability since both reduce a person's ability to function normally.

Yet learning the diagnosis of cancer may have a unique anxiety-bearing capacity since it possesses similarities to the widely feared unconscious: its occurrence is unexpected and seemingly irrational, apparently arising from nowhere, and experienced as all-powerful.

But these are false since every unconsciously-derived act has a valid reason, even those which appear senseless. In one published case a surgeon felt compelled to expose himself on the street despite grave legal risk until psychotherapy revealed that, by doing so, he was boasting to his mother how powerful he was, as he had wished to do when a toddler.

A clergyman and three-time survivor of cancer advised that, when afflicted by serious illness: Pray, but get the best medical advice too!

WAS BARNARD COLLEGE RESPONSIBLE FOR THEIR STUDENT'S MURDER?

The murder of eighteen-year-old Barnard College student, Tessa Majors, during an armed robbery in a nearby park at nightfall, was shocking but unsurprising. Common sense is that one should not walk at that time in that place.

My statement is not meant to place blame on the unfortunate victim but rather to assert that Barnard should have educated its students, many of whom are new to New York City, about City ways. Or, in other words, given them "street smarts."

Would doing this have saved Tessa's life? Perhaps not since teenagers can be impulsive. But, having done so, Barnard's administrators might now sleep easily.

WHY MOST TEACHERS FAIL WITH PROBLEM STUDENTS

Teachers are generally clueless about interacting with problematic students and for good reason: because it's not their job!

Most learning problems derive from inadequate early parenting which affects the development of basic ego capacities governing behavior and thinking. Limitations exacerbated by parents who didn't first read to and then with their toddlers, who bossed them around rather than explaining "why" (which depresses the development of the capacity for abstract thinking), and who didn't foster their individual development and demand civil behavior.

All else is window dressing, like the schoolhouse computer software which is expected to alleviate early life failings but can't. Thus teachers are blamed for being unable to *re-parent* their students, which is not their job and a complicated lengthy business too.

ANXIETY DISORDERS AND THE CURRENT RETREAT FROM RELATING TO UNCONSCIOUS MOTIVATION

Doctors often discuss treatment of the supposed "anxiety epidemic" in terms of genetics and medications, even with the newly marketed Transcranial Magnetic Stimulation. In one well-reviewed book the author described her multiple fears and the neurotic and psychotic symptoms of her parents and grandparents, yet slighted her early therapist who asked if she was angry with her father.

Despite the scary headlines, anxiety disorders are generally easily treated. Though, like all psychological symptoms, they are painful and frightening since they can cripple a person's Executive Function which governs behavior.

Even the more greatly feared Panic Disorder merely reflects the experience of severe anxiety during which the symptoms of anxiety are *misinterpreted* as a deadly medical event. Many people rushing to an Emergency Room, fearing that they are suffering a cardiac event, are in the throes of a psychological not medical crisis.

As I often insist: the unconscious is very powerful and one must respect its power.

EIGHT TRUTHS FOR THE NOVICE PSYCHOTHERAPIST

(1) Progress in therapy isn't correlated with the amount of talking.

(2) A therapist usually becomes nervous when there is something important they missed.

(3) New patients usually know what they should do but can't.

(4) Know someone well enough, by questioning them on the phone, before accepting them as a patient lest you regret it afterward.

(5) The initially troublesome patient can turn out to be great.

(6) It's painful to begin therapy so respect your new patient's courage.

(7) Don't expect gratitude from patients even from those who, figuratively, owe you their life or, literally, their marriage.

(8) Respect the power of the unconscious but also the possibility of reducing your patient's troublesome behavior and painful feelings through accurate interpretations of its machinations.

DOCTORS FEAR PSYCHOTHERAPY TOO!

One surgeon's life became so consumed by anxiety that she stopped working. While anxiety and particularly panic attack can commonly disable, what is revealing is why this doctor resisted seeking mental health treatment: because a psychiatrist would place her on medication that reduced her technical skills. Which was likely true since this is the only treatment that almost all psychiatrists offer.

Today's psychiatry residents receive only ten-percent of the training in psychotherapy that they received seventy-years ago. But other mental health professionals are available as are the few psychiatrists who underwent psychoanalytic training and practice psychotherapy.

Yet this doctor's story tells another important lesson: that fear of the unconscious is widespread for even among doctors the unconscious is very powerful.

TREATING PTSD WITH HYPNOSIS

While a hospital administrator, I developed pain in my neck at the end of each day, soon interpreting this as reflecting some of my employees being a pain in the neck which they were. Having had training in hypnosis, I used a research protocol from a journal article to make a ten-minute self-hypnotic relaxation audio. After listening to it twice my neck pain disappeared.

Years later when a nurse at another stressful job found my blood pressure high. I began using this audio (which was now a CD) several times a day. Within two months my blood pressure readings decreased to optimal and have remained so.

I'm a great believer in the efficacy of hypnosis, not considering it a learned reaction as do some researchers but that it fosters entrance into a different physiological state, having experienced this *drop* during its induction. Napping while using a self-hypnotic audio is more restful too with a short nap feeling like several hours of sleep upon awakening.

I use this audio daily and offer it to my adult patients for relaxation though hypnosis is helpful for more. It is used: to alleviate the pain of childbirth, burns, and back ache; to lower high blood pressure; to reduce sleep difficulty, to ease the stress of asthmatic children so they're less likely to have an asthma attack, and more.

Overall, apart from relieving concurrent stress and anxiety, I believe that hypnosis is less useful in eliminating specific trauma such as from a recent airplane crash. Here, education of the nature of trauma and psychodynamic interpretation of its residue would benefit more.

Hypnosis is also safer than medication which can have wide-ranging side effects.

EXPLAINING SUICIDE

Rather than being a mystery, suicide reflects deep long-existing feelings of worthlessness exacerbated by immediate stress. Thus, a teenager doesn't suicide simply because they broke up with their boy or girl friend, and most current American soldiers who committed suicide never saw combat with many never having left the USA.

Substance abuse is the attempted self-medication of despair. It's not easy to kill oneself, living being a biological imperative, unless one momentarily lacks self-control because of drug or alcohol use.

To paraphrase F. Scott Fitzgerald, 3AM is the darkest time of the day. Nelson Algren attempted suicide after the sales failure of his first novel in 1935. Fourteen years later he posthumously won the National Book Award for *The Man With the Golden Arm*.

As has long been said, suicide is a permanent solution to a temporary problem.

THE PATHOLOGICALLY OBSESSIVE BOSS

Obsessive CEO's are common because their talents for orderliness and control foster authority and clear decision making. But they have a downside too since a too-great need for order strengthens bureaucratic elements, fostering decision-making based on rules rather than staff creativity and autonomy.

While clear, followed rules can protect against an organization's political struggles, it encourages the passive resistance of staff and fosters the misuse of resources.

Moreover, unresolved sadistic elements of a leader's obsessive personality can cause them to be obstinate and vengeful, battling their corporate opponents into submission which devastates functioning and is especially harmful during periods of rapid industry change.

EXPLAINING SCHOOL BULLYING

Though all agree that bullying is bad, its complexity is often downplayed. Factually, bullies may primarily be sadistic, depressed, or anxious; and victims may primarily be submissive, provocative, or masochistic. Varying teacher and family dynamics exist for each ranging from fear and helplessness to parents who gain vicarious satisfaction from their child's asocial behavior.

Successful intervention requires both accurate diagnosis of the underlying dynamics and that both school and family share the same goal, which is often not easy. Ideally, intervention would begin in pre-school since the later it occurs, the greater will be the effort needed to affect change.

THE FEAR OF "GOING CRAZY"

The part of the mind that controls behavior is termed the *Executive Function*. There are few greater fears than its loss. of "going crazy," since one could not function adequately with having a locus of control.

This common fear is almost always unjustified since, when arising, it is usually with those whose sense of self, sense of who they are, is tied to *excessive* self-control. Thus a loosening of their defensive pattern threatens the loss of sensing who they are, which may be incorrectly self-diagnosed as "falling apart" or "having a breakdown."

The actual "going crazy" is not easy and arises only after enduring long-term excessive stress, or substance abuse.

WHEN POST-TRAUMATIC STRESS DISORDER (PTSD)
SYMPTOMS FEEL WORSE

While nightmares and flashbacks are frightening enough, another symptom is worse: agitated/anxiety-laden depression which seems never-ending. This feeling of being alone and helpless originates in infancy, a period when the child is completely dependent on their parents for survival.

Slowly, the child's mind creates an image of an all-nurturing parent who, when inevitably absent for periods of time, will *always* return to supply their needs. When this feeling of absolute helplessness and isolation becomes associated with PTSD, it makes its common symptoms feel even worse.

BEING UNLOVED AT BIRTH

A patient rejected my interpretation of their nightmare as indicating anger toward their birth-mother for her lack of affection. "No, my mother *always* loved me," she said emphatically. Which may have been true since the mother's relinquishing of parental rights enabled the patient's life to dramatically improve after their adoption and psychotherapy.

It is hard to accept being unloved at birth. Though the helpless infant can survive without physical care, psychological neglect can equally damage their future. And the most important person in their earliest years is their mother, or a mothering figure who can also be a male, some fathers being the "motherly" figure in the family..

Viewing the world with an immature mind, every child considers their parents omniscient. Thus if the child is unloved, they believe it to be *their* fault. Only with maturity and possibly psychotherapy can one accept a basic psychological truth: that while all children are lovable at birth, some mothers are incapable of providing love. But for this realization to occur, two things must happen: their own psychological maturation, and an acceptance of their and their parent's limitations.

HOW TO SURVIVE A TERRIBLE BOSS (AND WHEN TO FIRE YOURSELF)

I once treated a young woman ("Ellen") who, while attending college, worked as a secretary for a media company. This was back in that nearly historic time when all executives had an assistant. Her boss was the archetype of a terrible boss, screaming so often that no one could tolerate working with him for long. But his behavior didn't bother Ellen who simply tuned out his railing and, before leaving the job, was asked to educate her replacement on how to cope with him.

The survivor of a painful childhood, Ellen had fled her family and briefly lived in her car. A college teacher, after learning her situation, accepted Ellen as a boarder until she graduated. This teacher also provided the good parental experience that Ellen lacked and gave her the ability to tune out her nasty boss.

After experiencing several stressful jobs, I came to the important conclusion that while choosing the right job is important, it's even more important to know when to leave it and my suggestions follow.

Quit your job, if you have the economic freedom to do so, at the following times.

1. When you can no longer tune out the boss' behavior, keeping in mind that not every comment deserves a reply and not replying often indicates greater strength.

2. When political infighting becomes intolerable. This is an individual matter since what one person considers intolerable, another person can manage. A helpful older (1980) book that I found useful is, *Office Politics (Seizing Power, Wielding Clout)*, by Marilyn Moats Kennedy.

3. When you develop psychosomatic symptoms such as stomach distress or neck pain. During one management job I accurately interpreted my neck pain, which I never previously experienced, as reflecting my employees being "a pain in the neck."

4. When your boss wants you to stay. If remaining too long in some management positions, you'll become viewed not as part of the solution, as you were initially, but as part of the remaining problems.

5. Finally: leave the job on friendly terms without harsh words since if a job was bad you were dumb to take it so that doesn't say much about you (Disclaimer: I've been dumb).

WHY PATIENTS LIE TO THEIR THERAPIST

A popular belief is that patients always tell the truth to their therapists but this isn't true.

1. A woman was referred by her internist to a psychologist for "counseling," the doctor's unspoken motive being that that the patient was a troublesome hanger-on in her office and to get her from there into my office. That the patient was likely dying was obvious from her appearance. A later telephone conversation between the psychologist and the internist revealed that virtually everything this courteous, charming patient said was a lie. Her continuing behaviors (smoking, alcohol use) injured her health and she had no interest in changing.

2. A teenager was placed in foster care after telling the Child Protective Services' worker that her mother beat her. She also said this in her court-ordered teenage girls' therapy group. Several months later the CPS worker phoned the psychologist to ask their opinion and was informed that the doctor had no reason to question the girl's assertion. Only later did the girl confess her lie: that her mother *hadn't* beaten her. She had stayed overnight with her boyfriend and made up the story from fear of her mother's wrath.

Why do people lie to their therapist and their lie take a particular shape? Attempting to make sense of their existence, all people create stories of their life based on memories. Some are accurate, some are exaggerated, and others are false though their story may be *felt* as if true many years later.

TEENAGERS AREN'T ALWAYS AS THEY SEEM

Near Huntington, Long Island's railroad station is a lovely low-income housing development. A young teacher, walking to a student's home for a parent visit, saw three teenagers sitting on a stoop and became frightened because everyone knows how dangerous teenagers are. While anxiously passing them she heard one ask the others, "Do you think she sells vacuums?"

EXPLAINING THE FEAR OF FLYING AND OTHER PHOBIAS

Though varying in type and severity, fears (phobias) are a universal and helpful human condition: how the unconscious enables a too-stressed person to function. Stress that is caused by an emotional conflict or a feared insight that disturbs the person's ability to function normally on the job or at home or in school.

Thus if an adult has marital problems they can't confront, they may develop a fear of flying or driving across bridges. Similarly, a child may suddenly fear to sleep in their room and insist on sleeping downstairs on the sofa, their bedroom encapsulating their fear (being a phobia) which can be avoided by sleeping elsewhere.

A phobia's purpose is to encapsulate the anxiety, this enabling the troubled person to function normally so long as the feared object or activity is avoided. Which is a quicker solution than overcoming the conflict in psychotherapy since, though inconvenient, most people can choose to avoid flying or driving over bridges, and sleeping on the sofa isn't a great hindrance for a child though puzzling their parents.

The unconscious is powerful and one must respect its power.

THE HARDEST ELEMENT IN TREATING CHILDREN IN PSYCHOTHERAPY

Almost paradoxically, what can be most difficult in treating a child is not the child but their parents' resistance to treatment deriving from misconceptions: that long-term problems can be eliminated quickly; that the therapist will deprecate their parenting or try to control their lives; or from simple jealousy, as when the child values their therapy and their tantrums end quickly when their mother says they would visit the therapist that day.

But more difficult for a therapist to deal with is guilt over earlier parenting mistakes though these are never deliberate. Babies are not born with instructions, are inserted willy-nilly into a stable family unit, and possess varied difficulty in parenting.

Moreover, parents had their own early life experiences to survive and do their best. After recognizing their child's need for treatment and gaining it, *any* guilt that parents feel is undeserved.

POSTPARTUM DEPRESSION IN FATHERS

The term Postpartum Depression has usually been reserved for mothers. And who can wonder why since, after the birth of her child, the mother's life irrevocably changes. Her priority must now be the welfare of her child who wholly depends on her for existence.

But a study in the journal, *Pediatrics*, revealed that some men also become depressed after the birth of their child. Which is also understandable since they may become sleep deprived from their newborn's nightly wakefulness or irritated by its crying and continual need to be watched.

Another reaction of fathers may be to spank their child, which can change behavior only briefly and create a poorly functioning adult. Forty percent of the depressed fathers in the study admitted to spanking their infant as contrasted with thirteen percent of the fathers who weren't depressed.

More parenting education is needed, and mental health information too since these fathers' depression is caused both by the increased demands of their newborn and from not understanding what they are experiencing. Thus they feel conflicted over what they should be doing and give up, or mistakenly conclude they have emotional problems and *depress* their feelings. Which is why their experience is termed *depression*.

IS PEPPER STRAYING A CHILD EVER ACCEPTABLE?

A news article described an eight-year-old, second grade Colorado boy being pepper sprayed by police after he tore a sharp piece of wood from the wall and tried to stab their teacher with it. The ensuing debate revolved over whether the police behaved judiciously.

Is it *ever* proper to pepper spray a young child or to handcuff and arrest them as the police did in other publicized situations? To my surprise, I found myself agreeing with what the police did. To talk a child down from a tantrum is no simple matter especially when they behave violently.

Early in my career, while working in a private hospital for adolescents, the new Assistant Director suffered a broken nose when he placed himself between two arguing boys. The youth who accidentally broke his nose felt horrible but such incidents can happen. Here, the Assistant Director made a mistake: when trying to talk down a confrontation one should not place themselves in the middle of it (I'm speaking of verbal confrontations, physical fights requiring other measures to ensure safety).

So to expect the typical police office to cope only verbally with a potentially dangerous child is demanding something beyond their training. In the Colorado situation no one was hurt, which was the best outcome that could be expected. Moreover, the police response may well have helped the child psychologically since there is nothing more frightening to an out-of-control child than feeling no one can stop them.

IS YOUR CHILD "AUTISTIC" LIKE A WORLD-RENOWNED PHYSICIST WAS "SCHIZOPHRENIC"?

Newspapers and other reports often spotlight high rates of autism among children. One, in South Korea, asserted it being present in one of every thirty-eight, including some "highly functioning children." Such numbers provoke understandable alarm since autism cripples functioning and demands huge public and private expenditures.

Yet I question the accuracy of these statistics since, having long worked in many mental health settings, I have seen few children who could accurately be described as autistic, fewer than five of the most severely disturbed, self-mutilating type and fewer than ten with lesser symptoms. Moreover, young children whose behavior exhibit some autistic features can have these quickly disappear when provided conventional play psychotherapy.

I have spoken with many parents who were made anxious by school personnel though their child's difficulties were far from autism. Does your child have "awkward movements" or "seem to be in a world of their own"? These were some of the questions on the South Korea study though all young children exhibit such "symptoms" at times, as do all writers.

What is seen in many autism studies is the greater interest in child psychological development which is desirable, and a lack of sophistication about it which is not.

While parents rarely feel guilt when their child becomes physically ill, this is not true when they develop emotional problems. Autism is perhaps the most affected by this attitude since, in its severest form, it is as close to being incurable as any mental illness.

Recent infant research has confirmed what clinicians long suspected: that parent-child interaction plays an overwhelming role in its development. Yet, denial of this fact is widespread and expressed in the continued, failed attempts to relate autism to vaccines or pollution or whatever. Which is understandable since the sight of an autistic child horrifies and no parent wants to feel responsible for this.

All children have strengths and limitations, as do parents who had their own childhood struggles. A parent's personality must mesh with their unselected child and mismatches inevitably occur. Thus once a child's problem is recognized and professional help is sought, any parental guilt is undeserved.

So, parents, if anyone describes your child as "autistic," have them evaluated a second and even a third time. You and they deserve it. And keep in mind that J. Robert Oppenheimer, the eminent leader of the Manhattan Project which built the atomic bomb during World War Two, was diagnosed when young as "schizophrenic." Every nation would benefit from having more such "schizophrenic" members.

ORGANIZATIONAL DETERIORATON UNDER THE
SCHIZOID MANAGER

Authority is granted a manager because of organizational needs, to accomplish tasks using the leader's skills and experience. And, recognizing this, workers submit to the manager's authority.

But during stressful times, pathological characteristics can emerge in a manager. One of these is the schizoid feature of isolation during which the leader isolates themselves and gives minimally explicit instructions which causes uncertainty about who can make decisions.

Organizational chaos follows during which excessive caution and over-concern with organizational politics blossom. Novel, creative ideas and the clear expression of opinion are now considered risky, causing the business to falter.

THE POST-TRAUMATIC STRESS DISORDER (PTSD) PANIC OF SOLDIERS

The experience of panic, which often occurs in PTSD sufferers, is the feeling of confronting overwhelming danger even when none exists. The prototype for this is the infant's state of helplessness when feeling intense anxiety over which they have no control. During development, the healthy child learns to use their anxiety in a healthy manner: to recognize that it signals danger and the need for action to thwart it.

But the mind of the PTSD sufferer, one who has tolerated repeated actual dangers, has become hypersensitized to danger signals. So when reminder of a past danger is sensed, a noise or color or even an odor, their mind may immediately be thrown into panic, akin to throwing a lighted match on gasoline.

Now the panic mode of infancy resurrects and with it the feelings of overwhelming peril and helplessness. Thus the potential to develop PTSD and its panic are ingrained in the essence of being human.

HOW ABUSE VICTIMS FALL APART PSYCHOLOGICALLY (DECOMPENSATE)

Abuse victims fall apart psychologically (decompensate) in stages.

The victim first denies the reality of imminent danger with a stubbornness bordering on psychotic. When this defense fails, they tend to lose control of themselves.

As other people fail to help them, the victim becomes depressed and enters a state of resignation.

Finally, as all prospect of a different future disappears, flashbacks of past trauma occur and the victim abandons hope. Which is not easily breached without outside help or a lucky break.

Victims who have been are coerced into behavior which violates their moral code (as stealing) are at greatest peril.

A VERY CHRISTMAS TALE

In the era before cellphones while driving outside St. Louis, my car got stuck on a road's divider while making a turn.

It was early morning with no help or cars to be seen. As I stood beside it, a car finally appeared and stopped opposite mine. It held four huge guys and I regretted leaving my pistol at home.

The driver came over and asked what happened. "My car's stuck," I said nervously. After briefly speaking to his companions they came to my car, picked it up, and moved it back onto the road.

I wanted to pay the driver but he refused. "There's a revival meeting at St. Louis Stadium tomorrow night. Come," he said.

Then, without another word, my four angels drove off and vanished into the night.